# Jean-Ja
# Rousseau

By United Library

**https://campsite.bio/unitedlibrary**

# Table of Contents

# Disclaimer

This biography book is a work of nonfiction based on the public life of a famous person. The author has used publicly available information to create this work. While the author has thoroughly researched the subject and attempted to depict it accurately, it is not meant to be an exhaustive study of the subject. The views expressed in this book are those of the author alone and do not necessarily reflect those of any organization associated with the subject. This book should not be taken as an endorsement, legal advice, or any other form of professional advice. This book was written for entertainment purposes only.

# Introduction

Jean-Jacques Rousseau (1712–1778) was a renowned philosopher, writer, and composer from Geneva. His profound influence on the Age of Enlightenment and his contributions to political, economic, and educational thought continue to shape modern society. Rousseau's works, such as the Discourse on Inequality and The Social Contract, are considered foundational texts in political and social philosophy.

In his Discourse on Inequality, Rousseau delves into the origins and consequences of social inequality, challenging prevailing notions of human nature and the structure of society. The Social Contract explores the concept of a just society, emphasizing the importance of popular sovereignty and individual freedoms. These groundbreaking works have had a profound impact on political movements and revolutions, including the French Revolution.

Rousseau's literary accomplishments extend beyond philosophy. His novel Julie, or the New Heloise, published in 1761, played a pivotal role in the emergence of preromanticism and romanticism in fiction. This sentimental novel explores themes of love, passion, and societal norms. Emile, or On Education, published in 1762, is an influential treatise on educational philosophy, highlighting the significance of individual development within the framework of society.

In addition to his philosophical and literary pursuits, Rousseau's autobiographical writings provide deep insights into his personal experiences and thoughts. The posthumously published Confessions, composed in 1769, is recognized as a foundational work in the genre of autobiography. His unfinished work, Reveries of the Solitary Walker, written between 1776 and 1778, reflects the introspective and subjective style that would become characteristic of modern writing.

Jean-Jacques Rousseau's intellectual contributions continue to resonate today, as his ideas on equality, freedom, and the role of the individual in society remain highly relevant. This comprehensive book explores the life, philosophy, and literary achievements of Rousseau, shedding light on his enduring impact on political, social, and cultural discourse.

# Jean-Jacques Rousseau

Jean-Jacques Rousseau, born in Geneva on June 28, 1712 and died in Ermenonville on July 2, 1778, was a Genevan writer, philosopher and musician. Orphaned by his mother at an early age, his life was marked by wandering. Although his books and letters enjoyed great success from 1749 onwards, they also brought him into conflict with the Catholic Church and Geneva, forcing him to change residence frequently and fuelling his feelings of persecution.

In the literary sphere, Jean-Jacques Rousseau enjoyed great success with his epistolary novel *Julie ou la Nouvelle Héloïse* (1761), one of the best-selling works of the 18th$^{e}$ century. The work captivated readers with its pre-Romantic depiction of love and nature. In *Les Confessions* (written between 1765 and 1770, with posthumous publication in 1782 and 1789) and *Les Rêveries du promeneur solitaire* (written in 1776-78, published in 1782), Rousseau delves deeply into his innermost feelings. The elegance of Rousseau's writing led to a significant transformation of French poetry and prose, freeing them from the rigid standards of the Grand Siècle.

In the philosophical sphere, Rousseau's reading in 1749 of the question put out to competition by the Dijon

Academy: "Has the re-establishment of the sciences and arts contributed to purifying or corrupting morals?" provoked what is known as the "illumination of Vincennes". This led to the works that would leave Rousseau a lasting mark on the world of thought: *Discours sur les sciences et les arts (*1750), *Discours sur l'origine et les fondements de l'inégalité parmi les hommes* (1755) and *Du contrat social* (1762).

Rousseau's political philosophy is built around the idea that Man is naturally good and that society corrupts him. By "naturally good", Rousseau means that human beings in the state of nature have few desires, so they are fierce rather than wicked. It is interactions with other individuals that make human beings "bad", and lead to growing inequalities. To regain natural goodness, man must resort to the artifice of the social contract, and be governed by laws derived from the general will expressed by the people. For Rousseau, unlike Diderot, for example, the general will is not universal, but specific to a particular state or body politic. Rousseau was the first to confer sovereignty on the people. In this respect, he can be said to be one of the thinkers of democracy (and in particular of direct democracy), even if he is in favor of what he calls elective aristocracy or tempered government in the field of executive power.

Rousseau was critical of the political and philosophical thought developed by Hobbes and Locke. For him, political systems based on economic interdependence and interest lead to inequality, selfishness and, ultimately, bourgeois society (a term he was one of the first to use). However, if he is critical of Enlightenment philosophy, it is an internal critique. He does not want to return to Aristotle, ancient republicanism or Christian morality.

Rousseau's political philosophy exerted considerable influence during the revolutionary period, when his book The *Social Contract* was "rediscovered". In the longer term, Rousseau left his mark on the French republican movement, as well as on German philosophy. Kant's categorical imperative, for example, is permeated by Rousseau's idea of the general will. During part of the 20th$^{e}$ century, a controversy arose between those who felt that Rousseau was in some way the father of totalitarianism, and those who exonerated him.

According to Claude Lévi-Strauss, Rousseau was the first true founder of anthropology, not least because his universalism posed "in almost modern terms" the problem of the transition from nature to culture. Historian Léon Poliakov adds that Rousseau invited his contemporaries to travel to distant countries, in order to "study, not always stones and plants, but once men and customs".

His body was transferred to the Paris Pantheon in 1794.

# Biography

**Family and childhood**

In his biography of Jean-Jacques Rousseau, Raymond Trousson notes that the family originated in Montlhéry, near Étampes, south of Paris. Jean-Jacques' quadrisaïeul (great-great-great-grandfather), Didier Rousseau, left this town to escape religious persecution against Protestants. He settled in Geneva in 1549, where he opened an inn. Rousseau's grandson, Jean Rousseau, and his son David Rousseau (1641-1738), Rousseau's grandfather, worked as watchmakers, a respected and lucrative profession at the time.

Jean-Jacques Rousseau was born on June 28, 1712 at his parents' Grand-Rue home in Geneva's upper town. He was the son of Isaac Rousseau (Geneva, 1672 - Nyon, 1747), a watchmaker like his father and grandfather, and Suzanne Bernard (Geneva, 1673 - Geneva, 1712), herself the daughter of a watchmaker named Jacques Bernard. Both parents were citizens[ref. needed]. They married in 1704, after a first union had brought the two families together, Suzanne's brother Gabriel Bernard having married Isaac's sister Théodora Rousseau in 1699. A first son, François, was born on March 15, 1705, before Isaac left his wife and newborn son in Geneva to work as a watchmaker in

Constantinople. He stayed for six years, returning home in 1711 to have a second child with his wife, who died of puerperal fever on July 7, 1712, nine days after Jean-Jacques Rousseau's birth.

He spent his childhood raised by his father and his father's sister in the house on Grand-Rue where he was born. His childhood was marked by early reading of novels with his father and the continual mourning of his mother. Following an altercation with a fellow countryman, Isaac Rousseau fled to Nyon in the Vaud region on October 11, 1722, to escape justice. He never returned to Geneva, but kept in touch with his sons, notably Jean-Jacques, who made regular trips to Nyon and to whom he passed on his passion for books. He entrusted his offspring to his double brother-in-law Gabriel Bernard, a fortification worker living in the Saint-Gervais district of Geneva. The latter entrusted him to Pastor Lambercier's boarding school in Bossey, at the foot of the Salève, south of Geneva, where he spent two years (1722-1724) in the company of his cousin Abraham Bernard. His brother François left home at an early age, and his whereabouts are lost in the Freiburg im Breisgau region of Germany.

His uncle placed him in an apprenticeship with a clerk, then, given the child's lack of motivation, with a master engraver, Abel Ducommun. The apprenticeship contract was signed on April 26, 1725, for a period of five years. Jean-Jacques, who until then had enjoyed a happy, or at least peaceful, childhood, was now confronted with harsh discipline. Three years later, on March 14, 1728, returning late from a walk outside the city and finding the gates of Geneva closed, he decided to flee, for fear of being beaten again by his master, but not before bidding farewell to his cousin Abraham.

**Madame de Warens and her conversion to Catholicism**

After a few days of wandering, he took refuge in the care of Confignon's parish priest, Benoît de Pontverre. The parish priest sent him to stay with a Vaudoise from Vevey, Baroness Françoise-Louise de Warens, who had recently converted to Catholicism and was looking after candidates for conversion. Rousseau fell in love with the woman who would later become his guardian and mistress. The baroness sent him to Turin to the Spirito Santo hospice for catechumens, where he arrived on April 12, 1728. Although he claims in his *Confessions to* have resisted his conversion to Catholicism for a long time (he was baptized on April 23), he seems to have come to terms with it fairly quickly. For a few months, he lived in Turin as a semi-oisif, living off a few jobs as a lackey-secretary and receiving advice and subsidies from aristocrats and abbots to whom he inspired some compassion. It was during his employment with the

Countess de Vercellis that the episode of petty theft (theft of the pink ribbon belonging to the niece of Mme de Vercellis) occurred, for which he cowardly blamed a young cook, Marion, who was consequently dismissed.

Desperate to rise above his circumstances, Rousseau discouraged his protectors and set off again, light-heartedly, for Annecy to find the Baroness de Warens in June 1729. A shy, sensitive teenager, he was in search of feminine affection, which he found in the Baroness. He was her "little one", calling her "Maman", and became her factotum. His interest in music prompted her to place him with a choirmaster, M. Le Maître, in October 1729. But on a trip to Lyon, Rousseau panicked and abandoned Le Maître in the middle of the street, struck down by an epileptic seizure. He then spent a year wandering in Switzerland, giving his first music lessons in Neuchâtel in November 1730. In April 1731, he met a false archimandrite in Boudry, and became his interpreter until the swindler was quickly exposed.

In September 1731, he returned to Mme de Warens, now living in Chambéry. At her home, he met Claude Anet, a sort of valet-secretary who was also the mistress's lover. Mme de Warens was the source of much of his sentimental and amorous education. The ménage à trois worked well until Claude Anet died of pneumonia on March 13, 1734. "Maman" and Jean-Jacques moved to Les Charmettes for the summer and autumn. During these few years, idyllic and carefree according to his *Confessions*, Rousseau devoted himself to reading, drawing on the extensive library of M. Joseph-François de Conzié, with which he built "a storehouse of ideas". An avid walker, he described the joys of being in nature, the pleasures of strolling and daydreaming, to the point of being described as a "dromane". He worked in the administrative services of the land registry of the Duchy of Savoy, then as a music teacher for young girls from the Chambéry bourgeoisie and nobility. But his health was fragile. In September 1737, "Maman" sent him to consult a Montpellier professor, Dr. Fizes, about his heart polyp. It was during this trip that he met Madame de Larnage, twenty years his senior, mother of ten children and his true initiator to physical love.

Back in Chambéry, he was surprised to find a new convert and lover in Madame de Warens, Jean Samuel Rodolphe Wintzenried, and the ménage à trois resumed. In 1739, he wrote his first collection of poems, *Le Verger de Madame la baronne de Warens*, a grandiloquent poem published in 1739 in Lyon or Grenoble.

**First contacts with the world of French Enlightenment**

Rousseau entered the orbit of two major Enlightenment figures, Condillac and D'Alembert, when, in 1740, he found a job as tutor to the two sons of the Provost

General of Lyon, M. de Mably. The latter was the elder brother of Gabriel Bonnot de Mably and Étienne Bonnot de Condillac, both of whom would go on to literary careers. For the younger of the two sons, Rousseau wrote a *Mémoire présenté à M. de Mably sur l'éducation de Monsieur son fils*. Rousseau's exposure to Lyonnais society won him a number of friendships, notably that of Charles Borde, who introduced him to the capital. Chambéry was close by, and he was able to pay a few visits to "Maman", but the ties were weakened. After a difficult year with his young pupils, Rousseau agreed with M. de Mably to terminate the contract. After some reflection, he decided to try his luck in Paris.

In Paris, thanks to a letter of introduction to M. de Boze, he was introduced to Réaumur, who allowed him to submit to the Académie des Sciences a memoir presenting his system of musical notation. It envisaged the abolition of the staff and its replacement by a cipher system. The academicians were not convinced by the project, which they claimed was nothing new, having been invented by Father Souhaitty. Rousseau persisted, improved his project and had it published at his own expense, without the hoped-for success, under the title *Dissertation sur la musique moderne*. During this period, he made friends with Denis Diderot, who was just as little-known as Rousseau, and received advice from Father Castel. He frequented the salons of Madame de Beserval and Madame Dupin, whom he tried in vain to seduce. In 1743, she entrusted him with the education of her son Jacques-Armand Dupin de Chenonceaux.

In July 1743, Rousseau was hired as secretary to Pierre-François, comte de Montaigu, who had just been appointed ambassador to Venice. His knowledge of Italian and his zeal made him indispensable to an incompetent ambassador. He enjoyed the lively Venetian life: shows, prostitutes and, above all, Italian music. But his self-importance made him arrogant, and Montaigu dismissed him after a year. He returned to Paris on October 10, 1744. This short experience nevertheless enabled him to observe the workings of the Venetian regime, and it was then, at the age of 31, that his interest in politics was awakened. He then conceived the project for a major work entitled *Les Institutions politiques (Political Institutions),* which was to become the famous *Du contrat social (The Social Contract)*. He worked on it from time to time for several years.

He then moved to the Hôtel Saint-Quentin, rue des Cordiers, where he married a young linen maid, Marie-Thérèse Le Vasseur, in 1745. She brought him the affection he lacked. He married her civilly in Bourgoin-Jallieu on August 30, 1768. Jean-Jacques had to put up with not only a talkative wife, but also her family. Between 1747 and 1751, Jean-Jacques Rousseau gave birth to five children, who, perhaps at the insistence of Marie-Thérèse's mother, were placed with the Enfants-Trouvés, the public welfare organization of the time. He first explains that he cannot afford to support a family, then in Book 8 of the *Confessions*, he writes that he has handed his children over to public education as an act of citizenship, as a father, and as an admirer of Plato's ideal Republic. In the next book of the *Confessions*, he also writes that he made this choice mainly to remove his children from the influence of his in-laws, whom he considered harmful. This decision would later be criticized by Voltaire, when he posed as a pedagogue in his book *Émile*, and also by those he called the "coterie holbachique" (D'Holbach's entourage, Grimm, Diderot, etc.). However, some of his friends, including Madame d'Épinay before she fell out with him, had offered to adopt these children.

In May 1743, he began composing a ballet héroïque, *Les Muses galantes*, excerpts of which were performed in Venice in 1744. In 1745, Rameau listened to pieces from Les *Muses galantes* at a farmer-general's house, and judged that "some are by an apprentice, others by a plagiarist". For the Fontenoy victory, he contributes to the creation of the Voltaire-Rameau duo's comedy-ballet, Les *Fêtes de Ramire*, based on Voltaire's *La Princesse de Navarre,* with music by Rameau. From 1745 to 1751, he earned his living as secretary and tutor to the Dupins. His circle of friends included Dupin de Francueil, his mistress Louise d'Épinay, Condillac, D'Alembert, Grimm and, above all, Denis Diderot. In 1749, Diderot invited him to take part in the *Encyclopédie* project, entrusting him with the articles on music.

# Celebrity and torment

**First great works**

In 1749, the Académie de Dijon put the question "Has the progress of science and the arts contributed to corrupting or purifying morals?" up for competition. Encouraged by Diderot, Rousseau took part in the competition. His *Discours sur les sciences et les arts* (known as the *Premier Discours*), which argues that progress is synonymous with corruption, won first prize in July 1750. The work was published the following year, and its author immediately gained international fame. The speech provoked numerous reactions; no fewer than 49 observations or rebuttals appeared in two years, including those from Charles Borde, Abbé Raynal, Stanislas Leszczynski and Frédéric II, enabling Rousseau to refine his arguments in his responses and bringing him growing fame.

He then gave up his jobs as secretary and tutor to become independent, and made a living from his work transcribing musical scores; he adopted a physical attitude and dress more in harmony with the ideas developed in the *Discourse*. But it was these ideas that gradually alienated him from Diderot and the philosophers of the *Encyclopédie*.

On October 18, 1752, his one-act interlude, *Le Devin du village*, was performed before King Louis XV and La Pompadour at Fontainebleau. The opera was a success, but Rousseau refused to be presented to the king the following day, thereby refusing the pension he might have been awarded. Immediately afterwards, he performed his play *Narcisse*, to which Marivaux had made a few alterations.

The year 1752 saw the start of the Querelle des Bouffons. Rousseau joined the Encyclopedists in writing his *Lettre sur la musique française*, in which he asserted the primacy of Italian music over French music, and of melody over harmony, while also flaying Jean-Philippe Rameau.

In 1754, the Dijon Academy launched another competition, to which he responded with his *Discours sur l'origine et les fondements de l'inégalité parmi les hommes* (also known as the *Second Discourse*), which made him famous. In it, Rousseau defends the thesis that man is naturally good, and denounces the injustice of society. Like the *First Discourse*, the work provoked fierce controversy, notably from Voltaire, Charles Bonnet, Castel and Fréron. Without waiting for the outcome of the competition, he decided to return to Geneva, and not without paying a visit to his old friend, M$^{me}$ de Warens. Famous and admired, he was well received. In terms of ideas, Rousseau distanced himself from the atheistic encyclopedists who believed in progress, while he advocated virtue and love of nature. He remained a fundamental believer, but abjured Catholicism and returned to Protestantism, becoming a citizen of Geneva. However, he remained in the city for only a few months. On October 15, he was back in Paris.

**Great works of art and social integration**

Rousseau no longer addressed bourgeois society alone, like the court artists and scholars of previous centuries. He was constantly addressing a different audience, one that was different from that of the high society that haunted the literary salons. Gradually, his fame became "fatal", in his own words; the fame he had sought as a social weapon turned against him, and he became paranoid, confronted with the public figure that "Jean-Jacques" had become, the one people wanted to see and meet, and whose portraits were circulating . In April 1756, Madame d'Épinay placed the Hermitage, a small house on the edge of the Montmorency forest, at his disposal. He moved in with Thérèse Levasseur and her mother, and began writing his novel *Julie ou la Nouvelle Héloïse* and his *Dictionnaire de la musique*. At the request of M^me^ d'Épinay, he also began editing the works of the Abbé de Saint-Pierre. Early in 1757, Diderot sent Rousseau his drama *Le Fils naturel*, which contained the line "The good man is in society, only the bad man is alone". Rousseau took this line as a disavowal of his choices, and an initial quarrel ensued between the friends.

During the summer, Diderot had difficulty getting the *Encyclopédie* published in Paris. His friends Grimm and Saint-Lambert were enlisted in the Seven Years' War. They entrust their respective mistresses, Mme d'Épinay and Mme d'Houdetot, to the virtuous Rousseau. Jean-Jacques fell in love with the latter, leading to what was probably a platonic romance, but due to clumsiness and indiscretions, rumors reached the lover's ears. Rousseau successively accused his friends Diderot, Grimm and Mme d'Épinay, who turned their backs on him for good. Mme d'Épinay gave him notice to leave, and he had to leave the Hermitage in December. He moved to Montmorency, where he rented the house that would become his museum in 1898.

In his *Lettre à M. d'Alembert* (1758), he opposed d'Alembert's idea that it would be in Geneva's interest to build a theater, arguing that it would weaken citizens' attachment to the life of the city.

Isolated in Montmorency and suffering from the stone disease, he became gruff and misanthropic. However, he won the friendship and protection of the Maréchal de Luxembourg and his second wife. However, he remained jealous of his independence, which gave him time for intense literary activity. He completed his hugely successful novel *Julie ou la Nouvelle Héloïse*, and worked on his essays *Émile ou De l'éducation* and *Du contrat social*. All three works were published in 1761 and 1762, thanks to the complaisance of Malesherbes, then director of the Librairie. In *La Profession de foi du vicaire savoyard*, at the heart of *Emile*, Rousseau refutes both the atheism and materialism of the Encyclopedists and the dogmatic intolerance of the devout party. In *The Social Contract, the* foundation of political society is based on the sovereignty of the people and civic equality before the law, the expression of the general will. This last work inspired pre-revolutionary ideology. Although *Emile* and the *Social Contract* marked the pinnacle of Rousseau's thought, they also isolated their author. The Paris Parliament and Geneva authorities condemned them as religiously heterodox. Threatened with imprisonment by the Grand Chamber of the Paris Parliament in June 1762, he had to flee France alone, with the help of the Maréchal de Luxembourg; he was later joined by Thérèse. He avoided Geneva, taking refuge in Yverdon with his friend Daniël Roguin. While his condemnation in Paris was mainly for religious reasons, it was the political content of the *Contrat Social* that earned him the hatred of Geneva. Berne followed Geneva's lead and issued an expulsion decree. Rousseau had to leave Yverdon and went to Môtiers to live with Madame Boy de la Tour. Môtiers is located in the principality of Neuchâtel, under the authority of King Frederick II of Prussia. The latter agrees to grant hospitality to the outlaw.

**Confronting religion and Voltaire**

Rousseau's misfortunes did not mollify the philosophers, who continued to condemn him, notably Voltaire and D'Alembert. Physically, the stone disease made him suffer, and he had to be probed regularly. It was then that he adopted a long Armenian garment, more convenient for hiding his affliction. He returned to writing a melodrama, *Pygmalion,* then a sequel to *L'Émile, Émile et Sophie, ou les solitaires,* which remained unfinished.

*L'Émile* was placed on the Index in September 1762, and Christophe de Beaumont, Archbishop of Paris, issued an anathema against the ideas professed in *Le Vicaire savoyard*. Rousseau responded with *Lettre à Christophe de Beaumont,* published in March 1763, a libel directed against the Roman Church. However, his deliberately "anti-papist" tone did not calm the ardor of Geneva's Protestant pastors, who waged a muted battle against Jean-Jacques' friends, who sought in vain to rehabilitate him. Tired, Rousseau finally renounced his Geneva citizenship on May 12, 1763. In the meantime, he developed a passion for botany and published his *Dictionnaire de la musique*, the fruit of sixteen years' work.

The conflict became political with the publication of *Lettres de la campagne* by Jean Robert Tronchin, Attorney General to the Petit Conseil de Genève, to which Rousseau replied with *Lettres de la montagne*, in which he took a stand in favor of the Conseil général, representing the sovereign people, against the Petit Conseil's right of veto. The letters were published in December 1764, but were burnt in The Hague and Paris, and banned in Berne. Voltaire chose this moment to anonymously publish *Le Sentiment des citoyens*, in which he publicly revealed the abandonment of Rousseau's children. The pastor of Môtiers, Montmollin, who had welcomed Jean-Jacques on his arrival, then sought to excommunicate him with the support of the "Vénérable Classe de ses confrères de Neuchâtel". But Rousseau was protected by a rescript from Frederick II. However, he was seen as a seditious figure, and the population rallied by Montmollin became so threatening that, on September 10, 1765, Jean-Jacques took temporary refuge on Île Saint-Pierre on Lake Bienne, from where the Bernese government expelled him on October 24. Before leaving, Jean-Jacques Rousseau entrusted his friend Du Peyrou with a trunk containing all his papers (manuscripts, drafts, letters and copies of letters).

**Years of wandering**

From then on, Rousseau lived in fear of a plot against him, and decided to begin his autobiographical work as a form of vindication. He went to Paris, where he stayed in November and December 1765 at the Temple, which was granted extraterritoriality. Rousseau was also under the protection of the Prince de Conti, who allowed him to receive distinguished visitors. At the invitation of David Hume, attached to the British Embassy in Paris, he left for England on January 4, 1766. Thérèse later joined him. During his stay in England, his mental instability increased, and he became convinced that David Hume was at the center of a plot against him. It was at this time that a forged letter from the King of Prussia to Rousseau was circulating in Parisian salons. It was well-written, but uncharitable. The author was Horace Walpole, but Rousseau at first attributed it to D'Alembert, then suspected Hume of involvement in the plot. Hume had frequented the Encyclopedists in Paris, who may have warned him against Rousseau. Rousseau, hypersensitive and suspicious, felt persecuted. After a six-month stay in England, the break between the two philosophers was complete, with each justifying the other's actions in public writings, generating a veritable scandal in the European courts. Rousseau's enemies, chief among them Voltaire, were jubilant, while his friends, who had urged him to entrust his fate to Hume, were dismayed by the turn of events.

During his stay in England, from March 22 1766 to May 1[er] 1767, he stayed with Richard Davenport, who made his property at Wootton Hall in Staffordshire available to the citizen of Geneva. It was here that he wrote the first chapters of his *Confessions*. The way he treats Diderot and Friedrich Melchior Grimm in his writings attests to his paranoia.

In May 1767, still under threat of condemnation by Parliament, Rousseau returned to France under the assumed name of Jean-Joseph Renou, the maiden name of Thérèse's mother. For a year, he was lodged by the Prince de Conti at the Château de Trye, near Gisors in the Oise region. The stay was particularly distressing for Rousseau, who came to suspect his friends, including the loyal DuPeyrou who came to visit.

On June 14, 1768, he left Trye and spent some time wandering around Grenoble in the Dauphiné. Thérèse joined him in Bourgoin on August 29 and, for the first time, he presented her to the town's mayor as his wife. He took over her name and moved to the Monquin farm in Maubec. He decided to leave the Dauphiné on April 10, 1770, spent a few weeks in Lyon, and arrived in Paris on June 24, 1770, where he stayed at the Hôtel Saint-Esprit, rue Plâtrière.

In Paris, he survived by copying music scores. He organizes readings of the first part of the *Confessions* in private salons, before silent, embarrassed audiences, as this soul is laid bare. Fearing revelations from his former friends, M[me] d'Épinay had the readings banned by Antoine de Sartine, then Lieutenant General of Police.

In his *Considérations sur le gouvernement de Pologne (Considerations on the Government of Poland), he* condemned the Russian policy of dismantling Poland. This position further marginalized him, as most French Enlightenment philosophers admired Catherine II. He continued to write *Confessions* and began work on *Dialogues, Rousseau juge de Jean-Jacques*. Unable to publish them without incurring further persecution, he tried to place the manuscript on the altar of Notre-Dame, but the closed gate prevented him from reaching it. In desperation, he goes so far as to hand out tickets to passers-by justifying his position.

This was also the period when he was herboring, an activity he shared with Malesherbes, and which brought the two men closer together. He wrote a botany course for his daughter Madelon, *Lettres sur la botanique, for* M[me] Delessert. *Les Rêveries du promeneur solitaire*, an unfinished work, was written during his last two years, between 1776 and 1778. These last works were not published until after his death. By this time, he was also corresponding with the opera composer Gluck.

ROUSSEAU

# Deaths

In 1778, the Marquis de Girardin offered him hospitality in a pavilion on his estate at Château d'Ermenonville, near Paris, where the writer-philosopher died suddenly on July 2, 1778, of what appears to have been a stroke. Some speculated that it was suicide, creating controversy over the circumstances of the philosopher's death.

The day after his death, the sculptor Jean-Antoine Houdon molded his death mask. On July 4, the Marquis René-Louis de Girardin had the body buried on the estate's Île des Peupliers. The tomb hastily erected by the Marquis de Girardin was replaced in 1780 by the present funerary monument designed by Hubert Robert and executed by J.-P. Lesueur: a sarcophagus sculpted on all four sides with bas-reliefs depicting a woman breastfeeding and reading *Emile*, as well as allegories of liberty, music, eloquence, nature and truth. On the pediment, a cartouche from which hangs a garland of palms bearing Rousseau's motto "vitam impendere vero" ("devote your life to truth"). The north face bears the epitaph "Here lies the man of Nature and Truth". The philosopher quickly became the object of a cult, and his tomb is assiduously visited.

**His intellectual itinerary**

Rousseau's great sensitivity profoundly marked his work, and partly explains the quarrels that marked his life. David Hume said of him: "All his life he has done nothing but feel, and in this respect his sensibility reaches heights beyond anything I have seen elsewhere; it gives him a keener sense of suffering than of pleasure. He is like a man who has been stripped not only of his clothes, but of his skin, and has found himself in this state to fight with the coarse and tumultuous elements." Bertrand Russell added: "This is the most sympathetic summary of his character that is remotely compatible with the truth.

# Rousseau's philosophy in context

Rousseau never took a philosophy course. Self-taught, he became a philosopher through his reading, particularly that of his immediate predecessors: Descartes, Locke, Malebranche, Leibniz, the *Logic of Port-Royal* and the Jusnaturalists' . From the very first work that made him famous, *Discours sur les sciences et les arts*, Rousseau claimed not to be a philosopher by profession, and expressed his distrust of some of those who called themselves philosophers. In this connection, he writes:

"In all times, there will be men made to be subjugated by the opinions of their century, their country, their society: such is the strong mind and the philosopher today, who, for the same reason, would have been nothing but a fanatic at the time of the League. One should not write for such readers, when one wants to live beyond one's century."

Three aspects of Rousseau's thought are particularly noteworthy:

- First and foremost, Rousseau was the first major critic of political and philosophical thought as it developed from the late 17th[e] century onwards. In opposition to Bacon, Descartes, Locke and Newton, he argued that what they called "progress" was first and foremost a decline in virtue and happiness, and that the political and social systems of Hobbes and Locke, based on economic interdependence and interest, led to inequality, egoism and bourgeois society (a term he was one of the first to use);

- secondly, although Rousseau was a critic of the political and philosophical theory of his time, his criticism came from within. He doesn't want to return to Aristotle, ancient republicanism or Christian morality, for while he accepts many of the precepts of the individualist and empiricist traditions of his time, he draws different conclusions from them by asking different questions. For example: is the state of war of all against all primary, or is it merely an accident of history? Can human nature not be shaped to achieve a democratic state?
- finally, Rousseau was the first to believe that democracy is the only legitimate form of state.

In his political writings, Rousseau follows in Bodin's footsteps, interpreting him through "the philosophical and legal theory of modern natural law". For him, Grotius and Pufendorf, as well as Locke, made the mistake of thinking that passions were natural, whereas they are merely the products of history. For Rousseau, the necessary satisfaction of primary needs (food, shelter, etc.), which so permeates human history, tends to isolate people. It doesn't bring them closer together, as in Pufendorf, nor does it stir up their discord, as in Hobbes.

Taking a stand against Grotius and Hobbes, according to whom freedom can be alienated because life is first, Rousseau argues in *Du contrat social* that freedom is inalienable because life and freedom are synonymous. Similarly, whereas in Hobbes, the people are constituted by the terror of power, in Rousseau, the people are constituted by a social pact that underpins their political unity. Unlike Locke, Spinoza or Hobbes, for Rousseau, once the pact is made, the human being loses all natural rights. On this point, he opposes the natural law school of Pufendorf, Grotius, Burlamaqui and Jean Barbeyrac, who conceive of "political law as the law of civil societies". What Rousseau is looking for is not the law of civil societies, but the law of the State.

**The "illumination de Vincennes", the first two speeches and the Enlightenment**

In 1749, during a visit to Diderot, then imprisoned in Vincennes, Rousseau read in the *Mercure de France* that the Académie de Dijon had launched a competition on the following question: "Has the re-establishment of the sciences and arts contributed to purifying or corrupting morals?" This reading provoked in him what is usually referred to as the "illumination of Vincennes", an event that was to profoundly change the course of his life: "Suddenly," he wrote, "I felt my mind dazzled by a thousand lights; crowds of ideas presented themselves at once with a force and confusion that threw me into inexpressible turmoil".

In the text he wrote for this competition, Rousseau opposed Montesquieu, Voltaire and Hume, who saw modernity and the perfection of the arts and sciences as extremely positive. The citizen of Geneva starts the restoration of the arts "at the fall of Constantine's throne", i.e., at the fall of the Byzantine Empire, "which brought to Italy the debris of ancient Greece". Influenced by the thinking of ancient classics such as Titus Livius, Tacitus and Plutarch, Rousseau "draws up an indictment of modern society and artifice". His models among the ancients are Sparta and the Roman Republic, when it was "the temple of virtue" before becoming, under the Empire, "the theater of crime, the opprobrium of nations and the plaything of barbarians". The anti-model is the city of Athens in the century of Pericles, which he finds too mercantile, too focused on literature and the arts, all of which, in his view, lead to the corruption of morals.

Rousseau's thought revolves around three axes: the distinction between useful sciences and arts and those he considers useless, the importance accorded to genius, and the opposition to luxury, which corrupts virtue. On the first point, Rousseau gives the arts and sciences an unflattering origin: "Astronomy is born of superstition; eloquence, of ambition, hatred, flattery, lies; all of them, and morality itself, of human pride. The sciences and arts owe their birth to our vices. However, he distinguishes between the useful sciences and arts, those that deal with things and relate to trades, to the manual labor of men (in 18th[e] century France, manual labor was despised), and the abstract sciences and arts motivated solely by the pursuit of worldly success. For Rousseau, the important thing is virtue, the "sublime science of simple souls" whose principles are "engraved in all hearts" and whose laws we learn by listening to "the voice of our conscience in the silence of our passions".

In line with his conception of the link between art or science and virtue, Rousseau distinguishes between the genius, who does not allow himself to be corrupted by the world, and the mundane. Addressing Voltaire, he writes: "tell us, famous Arouet, how many strong male beauties you have sacrificed to your false delicacy, and how much the spirit of gallantry so fertile in small things has cost you in great ones". In general, he believes that the geniuses (Bacon, Descartes, Newton) have been able to focus on the essentials and have contributed to the improvement of human understanding: "it is to this small number that it belongs to build monuments to the glory of the human spirit".

Rousseau sees an antinomy between luxury, which he associates with commerce and money, and virtue: "Ancient politicians spoke incessantly of morals and virtue; ours speak only of commerce and money". For Rousseau, luxury leads to the development of inequalities and the depravation of morals. On this point, he was at odds with the major trend of his century, represented by the likes of Mandeville and Voltaire, who, in Le *Mondain,* argued in favor of the superfluous, as well as the physiocrats and David Hume, who saw luxury as a spur to economic activity. The citizen of Geneva, aware of this opposition, notes:

"Let luxury be a sure sign of wealth; let it even serve to multiply it: what should we conclude from this paradox, so worthy of being born in our day; and what will become of virtue, when we have to enrich ourselves at whatever price?"

***Discourse on the origin of inequality among men***

In 1755, Rousseau published *Discours sur l'origine et les fondements de l'inégalité parmi les hommes*. For Jean Starobinski, Rousseau's Discourse on the Origin and

Foundations of Inequality among Men "reconstructs a philosophical 'genesis' in which neither the Garden of Eden, nor guilt, nor the confusion of tongues are missing - a secularized, 'demythologized' version of the story of origins, but one which, by supplanting Scripture, repeats it in a different language".

Rousseau imagines what humanity might have been like when Man was good: a state of nature that may never have existed. This is what is known as a conjectural history, based on a conjecture, i.e. a hypothesis. On this basis, he explains how Man, naturally good, became bad. According to him, the Fall is not due to God (he assumes him to be good), nor to Man's nature, but to the historical process itself, and the political and economic institutions that emerged in the course of this process. For Rousseau, evil refers both to the torments of the spirit that so preoccupied the Stoics, and to what moderns call alienation, i.e. the extreme attention that human beings pay to the gaze of others. This attention distracts them from their innermost selves, their very nature.

Rousseau ends his speech by defining his vision of equality, in which inequality of conditions must be proportionate to inequality of talents, and by noting that Man cannot turn back the clock, that the state of nature is definitively lost.

**Change of life (1756-1759)**

During this period, Rousseau felt the need to change his life and follow the precept he would henceforth include in numerous texts "*vitam impedere vero* (devote your life to the truth)". First of all, he changed his clothes. I sold my watch, saying to myself with incredible joy: "Thank heaven, I won't need to know what time it is anymore"' . He also left the city to settle in the countryside, first at L'Ermitage in the Montmorency forest, then at the Petit Mont-Louis house. Finally, he refused the positions and pensions he was offered. To remain free, he earned his living as a music copyist. He also broke the strong bond that had existed between him and Diderot since 1742.

For Jean Starobinski, Rousseau's ostentatious poverty has a dual purpose. Firstly, it is a "demonstration of virtue in the Stoic or Cynic manner", designed to alert people's consciences to the high levels of social inequality prevailing at the time. It is also a demonstration of Rousseau's loyalty to his social origins. According to this author, Rousseau had the genius to adhere to a very Plutarchian principle, which he expressed in a letter to his father when he was only nineteen: "I value obscure freedom more than brilliant slavery"' .

### ***The Social Contract* and *Emile***

*Du contrat social* and *Émile ou De l'éducation* were both published in 1762. They were almost immediately condemned. In France, condemnation came from both the Parliament (Ancien Régime) and the Faculty of Theology. In Geneva, it came from the Petit Conseil. These condemnations had serious consequences for Rousseau, forcing him into a life of wandering. While the French Revolution contributed to making the *Social Contract* his most esteemed work in France, the German tradition preferred the *Second Discourse* and the *Emile*.

***The social contract***

Initially, Rousseau wanted to write a book entitled *Institutions politiques*. However, he abandoned this project because he felt it had already been dealt with by Montesquieu. He then set out to write a book that would focus on the nature of things, and thus provide a foundation for political law. Comparing Montesquieu's book with his own, he writes in *Émile*, "the illustrious Montesquieu ... was content to deal with the positive law of established governments; and nothing in the world is more different than these two studies". The aim of the *Social Contract* is to found both political law and the State. According to Mairet, what gives this work its unique status is that, in the manner of Plato, it "establishes from the outset the link between truth and freedom".

The notion of the *Social Contract is not to be* understood as a formal contract between individuals, but as the expression of the idea that "legitimate power to govern is not directly founded on a divine title or on a natural right to govern, but must be ratified ("authorized") by the consent of the governed".

In *Du contrat social,* Rousseau seeks to answer what he believes to be the fundamental question of politics: how to reconcile the freedom of citizens with the authority of the state, based on the notion of sovereignty that he takes from Bodin. For Gilles Mairet, the radical novelty of the *Social Contract lies in the* fact that it affirms both that the people are sovereign and that the republic is a democracy. In this work, Rousseau is determined to prevent human beings from being subjected to the arbitrariness of rulers, which is why, as he states in a letter to Mirabeau dated July 26, 1767, his aim is to "find a form of government that puts the law above men". Rousseau wanted to combine political idealism with anthropological realism. He writes: "I want to find out if, in the civil order, there can be any legitimate and safe rule of administration, taking men as they are and laws as they can be. In this search, I shall always try to combine what the law allows with what the interest prescribes, so that justice and utility are not divided.

The *Social Contract* comprises four books. The first two are devoted to the theory of sovereignty, and the last two to the theory of government.

### *Emile, or Education*

This work, begun in 1758 and published in 1762 at the same time as the *Social Contract,* is both one of the most important treatises on education and one of the most influential. It follows in the footsteps of Plato's *Republic* and Fénelon's *Adventures of Telemachus*, which combine politics and education (Rousseau particularly cites Plato's dialogue, presenting it as a work of education that should not have been judged by its title). There is little to motivate Rousseau to write a work on education. If he was tutor to the children of Mably (the brother of Condillac and Abbé de Mably), the experience seems to have been inconclusive. Moreover, as Voltaire was sure to point out, Rousseau abandoned his five children, born between 1746-1747 and 1751-1752, to the hospice des enfants trouvés, even though he encouraged parenthood (women to make children and fathers to take care of their children's education).

The work is based on Rousseau's fundamental conception that Man is born good, but society has corrupted him. Thus he posits as "an incontestable maxim that the first movements of nature are always upright: there is no original perversity in the human heart. There is not a single vice in the human heart of which we cannot say how and by which means it entered", . Rousseau divides the education of human beings into five phases, corresponding to the five books of Emile. Book I deals with newborn babies, Book II with children aged 2 to

10/12, Book III with 12- to 15/16-year-olds, Book IV with puberty, dominated by conflicts between reason and passions, while also tackling questions of metaphysics or religion in a section known as *La Profession de foi du vicaire savoyard (The Savoyard Vicar's Profession of Faith), which was* published separately. Finally, Book V deals with the young adult as he initiates himself into politics and takes a companion.

In line with his conception of the human person, education must first of all be *negative, i*.e. it must not begin by instructing, as this risks perverting human nature: "The first education must therefore be purely negative. It consists, not in teaching virtue or truth, but in securing the heart from vice and the mind from error". In his *Pensées sur l'éducation* (1693), Rousseau criticizes John Locke for wanting to consider the child as a reasonable being too early on, and for wanting to use education to transform the child into a man, rather than letting the child be a child, waiting for him to grow up and become an adult in the natural way. For Rousseau, it's only at puberty that education should provide moral training and enable the adolescent to integrate the social world.

# Rousseau and religion

Three groups of texts should be taken into account to understand Rousseau's relationship with religion:

- theoretical" or "dogmatic" writings, such as the *Lettre à Voltaire sur la Providence*; Book IV of *Emile,* entitled *Profession de foi du vicaire savoyard (Profession of Faith of the Savoyard Vicar*), added *at the last minute* to the work shortly before printing; the 8[e] and final chapter of the *Contrat social (Social Contract)*, also added at the last moment at the end of the book (chapter 8 is the longest in the entire work); and finally, *La Nouvelle Héloïse (The New Heloise)*. These last three works were published in the same period (1762-1763);
- justification or polemical writings: the *Lettre à Christophe de Beaumont*, the *Lettres écrites de la montagne* and the *Dialogues* (*Rousseau juge de Jean-Jacques*);
- private correspondence, including letters to Paul Moultou and the letter to Franquières from 1769.

Rousseau's Christian faith is a kind of rationalist deism, inherited from Bernard Lamy and Nicolas Malebranche:

there is a god because nature and the universe are ordered. Rousseau is no materialist (see *Letter to Franquières*), but he is neither an orthodox Protestant nor a Roman Catholic. Nevertheless, he claimed to be a "believer", including in his letter of February 14, 1769 to Paul Moultou, who seemed eager to renounce his faith, and whom he urged not to "follow fashion".

In particular, Rousseau did not believe in original sin, a doctrine that incriminated human nature and which he fought against at length. He speaks ironically of this sin "for which we are justly punished for faults we have not committed" (Mémoire à M. de Mably). He rejected this doctrine for theological reasons, as he saw in the implications of this dogma a harsh and inhuman conception, which "greatly obscures the justice and goodness of the Supreme Being"; but it was also because, feeling good, he could not conceive of being affected by a secret flaw. This position led him to forge the fiction of a "state of nature", extra-moral and extra-historical, to set aside all the facts of history.

**Rousseau himself**

By way of autobiography, Rousseau wrote three works: *Les Confessions*, *Rousseau juge de Jean-Jacques*, and Les *Rêveries du promeneur solitaire*, which he never completed.

*The Confessions* were written between 1763 or 1764 and 1770. Although Rousseau presents his past faults in this work, such as the episode involving the stolen ribbon, *Confessions* is less a confession in the Augustinian sense, than a kind of self-portrait à la Montaigne. The purpose of the book "is to make known exactly what I'm like inside, in all the situations of my life. It is the story of my soul that I have promised"' .

He wrote *Rousseau juge de Jean-Jacques between* 1772 and 1776. Partially published in 1780, the work caused some unease, as Rousseau denounced a conspiracy against him by Grimm, Voltaire, D'Alembert and David Hume. In it, Rousseau dialogues with Jean-Jacques, who represents the Rousseau as seen by his enemies, and a third character called "the Frenchman", who represents public opinion, i.e. someone who has neither met Rousseau nor read his books. This is the person he wants to convince.

*Les Rêveries du promeneur solitaire* was written between 1776 and 1778, until Rousseau's death. In this book, life is "constituted as a philosophical object", but contradictions are visible between his political project, which aims to integrate the citizen into political life, and Rousseau's deepest inclination. He writes "[...] I have never really been suited to civil society, where everything is a hindrance, an obligation, a duty, and [...] my independent nature has always made me incapable of the subjection necessary for those who wish to live with men"' .

The status of these texts poses a problem. For Alexis Philonenko, Rousseau's philosophy, "faced with the obstacle, retreated into a theory of individual existence". On the contrary, for Géraldine Lepan, these works "can be read as the necessary complement to the 'sad and great system' that emerged from the Illumination of Vincennes". The aim is always the same: "to reveal the self beneath social deformations".

# Rousseau's human nature and conjectural history

## Conjectural history

According to George Armstrong Kelly, Rousseau's approach to the puzzle of history is the most antithetical of all: moral. For Rousseau, history is both a collection of examples and a succession of states of human faculties that evolve according to the challenges of time. For the citizen of Geneva, history is never a point of departure, but rather a means of extending his own tension to humanity as a whole. The philosopher doesn't use data to question its meaning, he uses it to support his own convictions. In *Emile,* Rousseau defends the idea that our impressions of the past should be used for educational purposes, not to cultivate theoretical knowledge. On this point, he differs from Jean le Rond D'Alembert, who had a more objective view of history, which he saw as providing posterity with a dispassionate spectacle of vices and virtues. In contrast, Rousseau writes in his *Histoire de Lacédémone*:

"I care very little if I am reproached for having lacked that grave coldness recommended to historians [...] as if the main utility of history were not to make all its good people love with ardor and the bad ones detest."

For Jean Starobinski, in a way, Rousseau's conjectural history aims to propose an alternative history to that of Christianity. Starobinski notes that, in the *Second Discourse,* "Rousseau reconstructs a philosophical 'genesis' in which neither the Garden of Eden, nor guilt, nor the confusion of tongues are missing. It's a secularized, "demythologized" version of the story of origins, but one that, by supplanting Scripture, repeats it in a different language. In this way, the state of nature can be seen as an imaginary reconstruction that replaces the biblical myth of the Garden of Eden in the Book of Genesis. At the beginning of the V$^{e}$ century, the expulsion of men from Eden - for having eaten of the forbidden fruit of the tree of the knowledge of good and evil - had inspired the Christian theologian Augustine of Hippo to the doctrine of original sin. Although he rejected this doctrine, Rousseau refers to it explicitly in note 9 of the *Second Discourse*.

For Victor Goldschmidt, Rousseau radicalized the conjectural method used by his contemporaries by taking the existence of the state of nature as a given. His main problem is to explain the transition from this natural state to civil society by purely natural causes, based on physical (health and biological equality), metaphysical (perfectibility and purely virtual freedom) and moral (self-love, pity and love) conjectures.

**From the state of nature to civil or political society**

Like Thomas Hobbes and John Locke and other thinkers of the time, but unlike Plato, Aristotle, Augustine of Hippo, Nicolas Machiavelli and others, the starting point of Rousseau's philosophy is the state of nature. But Rousseau didn't consider the tribesmen of his time in America to be in a state of nature: for him, they were at a more advanced stage. To think of human beings in their natural state, we have to go back further and imagine something that may never have existed. Rousseau writes that he will consider the human being "as he must have come from the hands of Nature", and in so doing, he writes, "I see an animal less strong than some, less agile than others, but all things considered, organized most advantageously of all".

According to Victor Goldschmidt, there is first of all a transition from the natural state to natural society, which he also calls the "youth of the world", without any "foreign impulse", simply because "the movement imparted to the state of nature continues of its own accord". On the other hand, the transition from natural to civil society can be explained by several foreign impulses.

Firstly, the development of agricultural and metallurgical techniques led to the appropriation and division of tasks. In addition, extraordinary natural phenomena such as volcanic eruptions changed the physical environment in which people lived. All these upheavals lead to an exacerbation of human passions. So, to avoid the worst, man must make an unnatural decision and enter into a social contract. For Jean Starobinski, the transition from the state of nature to the civil society of the pre-social contract era takes place in four phases:

1. the idle man living in a scattered habitat who gradually associates in a horde;

2. the first revolution: humanity enters the patriarchal order, and families are able to join together. For Rousseau, this was the golden age;

3. the patriarchal order gave way to a world marked by the division of tasks that made men lose their unity. The most violent or the most skilful become the rich and the others the poor;

4. the war of all against all, understood by Rousseau in a Hobbesian sense.

At the end of this process, the establishment of a social contract makes it possible to emerge from the state of war and achieve a civil society marked by inequality. As Jean Starobinski writes: "stipulated in inequality, the contract will have the effect of consolidating the advantages of the rich, and of giving inequality the value of an institution". In *Du contrat social,* Rousseau seeks a way out of this first unequal social contract through the concept of the general will, which will enable, in Christopher Bertam's words, "each person to benefit from the common force while remaining as free as they were in the state of nature". In short, for Rousseau, the State is the way out of the evil of society. For Victor Goldschmidt, the opposition between the contract of the *Discourse* and that of the *Social Contract* should not be overemphasized, since in both, inequality is present.

Victor Goldschmidt notes in *Anthropologie et Politique* (pp. 779-780) that Rousseau "discovered social constraint, the [...] social [...] relationship, the autonomous life and development of structures [...], their independence from individuals and, correlatively, the web of dependence of these same individuals on these structures".

**Self-love and pity or the end of the naturally good man**

Rousseau repeats on several occasions that the idea that man is naturally good, and that society corrupts him, dominates his thinking. The question that then comes to mind is: how can evil arise in a society made up of good men? The adjective "good" does not mean that men were originally naturally virtuous and beneficent, but, according to John Scott, that in man "there would originally exist a balance between needs and passions and the capacity to satisfy them", and it would be this balance that would make man "good for himself and not dependent on others", for it is precisely "dependence on others that makes men evil".

Rousseau argues that, in order to preserve the species, creatures are endowed with two instincts: self-love and pity. Self-love enables them to satisfy their biological needs, while pity leads them to care for others. It should be noted that, while pity is an independent instinct in the *Second Discourse*, in the *Emile* and the *Essay on the Origin of Languages*, it is seen only as an extension of self-love, seen as the origin of all passions.

The fall, or evil, is introduced in man with the emergence of self-love, an emergence, moreover, linked to sexual competition to attract a partner. Rousseau writes in note 15 of his *Discourse on the Origin of Inequalities*:

In short, self-love drives human beings to compare themselves, to seek to be superior to others, and this leads to conflict. However, if we look at his treatment of the issue, starting with *Emile, we* can see that self-love is both the instrument of man's downfall and of redemption. Indeed, in this book, self-esteem is the form taken by self-love in a social environment. While Rousseau always sees self-love as dangerous, it can be contained through education and good social organization, as outlined in *Emile* and the *Social Contract* respectively.

Even if self-love is rooted in sexual competition, it only reveals its full potential for danger when combined with the economic interdependence that develops when individuals live in society. In this case, human beings seek both material goods and recognition, leading to social relationships marked by the subordination of some and by the desire to achieve one's ends, whatever the means employed. As a result, both the freedom of human beings and their self-esteem are threatened.

**Passions, reason and perfectibility**

Unlike Aristotle, but like Thomas Hobbes and John Locke, for Rousseau reason is subordinate to the passions, particularly self-love. What's more, the passions and reason evolve and have their own dynamic. Initially, in the state of nature, human beings have few passions and little reason. Rousseau notes, concerning men in the state of nature (whom he calls savages) that they "are not wicked precisely because they do not know what it is to be good; for it is neither the development of enlightenment, nor the restraint of the Law, but the calm of the passions and ignorance of vice that prevents them from doing wrong". The dynamic of passions and reason that leads to their evolution is made explicit by Rousseau in the following passage:

"Whatever the Moralists may say, human understanding owes much to the Passions, which, by common admission, also owe much to it: it is through their activity that our reason is perfected; we seek to know only because we desire to enjoy, and it is not possible to conceive why he who had neither desires nor fears would take the trouble to reason. Passions, in their turn, derive their origin from our needs, and their progress from our knowledge; for we can desire or fear things, only on the ideas we can have of them, or by the simple impulse of Nature; and the savage man, deprived of every kind of light, experiences only Passions of the latter kind."

For Rousseau, the dominant trait of man is not reason, but perfectibility. Speaking of the difference between human beings and animals, Rousseau writes: "There is another very specific quality which distinguishes them, and on which there can be no dispute, and that is the faculty of self-perfection; a faculty which, with the help of circumstances, successively develops all the others, and resides among us as much in the species as in the individual, instead of an animal being, after a few months, what it will be all its life". While Rousseau is one of the first, if not the first, to use the word perfectibility, for him, the word does not have only a positive aspect. On the contrary, it often had a negative aspect. Indeed, for the citizen of Geneva, perfectibility is merely the ability to change, an ability that most often leads to corruption.

### Virtue and conscience

According to Georges Armstrong Kelly, "Rousseau refers to 'wisdom' as the seat of virtue, the consciousness that does not create light, but rather activates man's sense of cosmic proportions". For Rousseau, moral truth is the unifying element of all reality. Knowledge is a false light, a mere projection of self-love, if it is not rooted, as it is for him, in an inner certainty. Otherwise, reason can be corrupted by the passions and transformed into false reasoning that flatters self-love. If reason can provide access to truth, only conscience, which imposes the love of justice and morality in an almost aesthetic way, can make us love it. The problem, for him, is that conscience based on a rational appreciation of an order traced out by a benevolent God is a rare thing in a world dominated by self-love.

### Political philosophy

Rousseau's political philosophy is set out in *Discours sur l'origine et les fondements de l'inégalité parmi les hommes, Discours sur l'économie politique, Du contrat social* and *Considérations sur le gouvernement de la Pologne*. Rousseau's political philosophy is rooted in the contractualist perspective of the British philosophers of the 17th$^{e}$ and 18th$^{e}$ centuries. Indeed, his *Discourse on Inequality* is sometimes seen as a dialogue with the work of Thomas Hobbes. For Christopher Bertram, the heart of

Rousseau's political doctrine lies in the assertion that "a state can be legitimate only if it is guided by the general will of its fellow citizens".

# A few important words from Rousseau's political philosophy

The general will is the key concept in Rousseau's political philosophy. But this expression is made up of two terms - will and generality - whose meaning needs to be clarified if we are to fully understand the thinking of the citizen of Geneva.

For Rousseau, as for all the "voluntarists" who came after Augustine of Hippo's book *On Free Will, the* will must be free to have any moral value. Freedom is first and foremost understood as non-submission to the authority of other men, as in the case of paternal power or the power of the strongest. However, Rousseau doubts that the will alone can lead men to morality. In his view, men need either great legislators like Moses, Numa Pompilius (Rome) or Lycurgus (Sparta), or educators to guide the will towards the good while remaining free.

For Rousseau, to say that the will is general means that it lies somewhere between the particular and the universal, as in Pascal, Malebranche, Fénelon or Bayle. According to

Patrick Riley, this vision of the "general" is "quite distinctly French". On this point, Rousseau is at odds with Diderot, who, in the *Encyclopédie* article "Droit naturel", develops the idea that there is both a general will of the human race and a universal morality, leading him to think of the general in universal terms. Rousseau, on the other hand, whose models are Rome, Sparta and Geneva, insists on the importance of national particularities.

Rousseau was not the first to combine the words "general" and "will" and use the expression "volonté générale": before him, Arnauld, Pascal, Malebranche, Fénelon, Bayle and Leibniz had also used it. But they used it to designate the general will of God, whereas for Rousseau, it refers to the general will of citizens. In short, the philosopher secularized and democratized the expression.

**Interpretations of the notion of the general will**

For Christopher Bertram, the general will in Rousseau is an ambiguous notion that can be interpreted in two ways: in a democratic conception, it is what the citizens have decided; in a more transcendent conception, it is the embodiment of the general interest of the citizens obtained by disregarding particular interests. The first interpretation is based primarily on chapter 3 of Book 2 of *Du contrat social*, where Rousseau insists on deliberative procedures to achieve the general interest.

It is possible to unify these two views by assuming that, for Rousseau, under the right conditions and with the right procedures, citizens will ensure that the general will resulting from deliberation corresponds to the transcendent general will. But for the citizen of Geneva, this identity is not assured. In this regard, he writes:

"It follows from the foregoing that the general will is always upright and always tends towards public utility: but it does not follow that the deliberations of the people are always of the same rectitude. We always want our good, but we don't always see it (*Du contrat social* livre II, chapitre III, p. 56)."

Believing that the quality of citizens' deliberation, once they are sufficiently informed, is jeopardized by the effects of rhetoric and simple communication between citizens, he asserts that Athenian democracy was in reality "a very tyrannical aristocracy, ruled by 'scholars' and 'orators'".

**Law and natural law**

In his *Discourse on Inequality,* Rousseau argues that natural law can be understood in two very different ways. For Roman jurisconsults, natural law expresses "the expression of general relationships established by nature between all animate beings, for their common preservation". For modern jusnaturalists, law is "a rule prescribed to a moral being, i.e. one that is intelligent, free and considered in its relations with other beings"; it is natural in the sense that it pursues man's natural ends, on which, according to Rousseau, the philosophers of his time hardly agreed. If there were such a thing as natural law, he concludes, it would have to meet both of the above definitions, which he considers impossible. For while men in the state of nature acted spontaneously with a view to the common good, this is no longer the case with modern man. So, according to Gourevitch, when Rousseau uses the term "natural law", he is not referring to his own views, but to those of modern jusnaturalists. When setting out his views, Rousseau prefers to speak of "natural law", for at least two reasons: law is generally understood as the expression of a command from a superior to an inferior, not right; moreover, right can be applied differently according to circumstances.

The problem for Rousseau is that, while self-love and pity drive human beings to follow natural law, as economic interdependence develops, self-love becomes self-love, and the law of human nature ceases to ensure respect for natural law. This observation leads Rousseau to state his "central thesis [that] once men have become irreversibly dependent on one another, spontaneous - 'natural' - conformity to natural law cannot be restored on a global scale".

## Political law and justice

Rousseau differentiates between natural law and political law. The latter refers to the principles or laws of what he often calls "well-constituted states". Political law aims, within the framework of a state or body politic, to positively establish a society that enables men to live well. It's not a question of returning to the state of nature, but of being able to lead a good life. To achieve this, political law, aided by instrumental reason, must enable a return to a certain form of justice. This leads Rousseau to distinguish three types of justice: "divine justice", "universal justice" and "human justice". The first comes from God; the second refers to Diderot, who, in the article "Droit naturel" in the *Encyclopédie* (IC, 2), sees law and justice as a pure act of reason; the third comes from Rousseau. For him, the idea of justice refers to a body politic and does not extend to the whole world. Rousseau notes in this regard:

"What is good and conforms to order is so by the nature of things and independently of human conventions. All justice comes from God, he alone is its source; but if we knew how to receive it from so high a source, we would need neither government nor laws. Undoubtedly, there is a universal justice emanating from reason alone; but this justice, to be accepted among us, must be reciprocal. If we consider things humanly, in the absence of natural sanction, the laws of justice are vain among men; they only do good to the wicked and harm to the just, when the latter observes them with everyone and no one observes them with him. Conventions and laws are therefore needed to unite rights with duties and bring justice back to its object."

# Body politic and citizenship

### Political society, civil society and political law

According to Rousseau, political society is not natural, and for him, man is not a political animal like Aristotle. The body politic that emerges from the convention and consent of its members enables the aggregation of resources and the pooling of the forces and resources of the society's members. To designate this body politic, Rousseau also uses the terms société bien constituée, "peuple", République, "État when it is passive, Souverain when it is active, puissance en comparant à ses semblables". The end or goal of a body politic is to propose a means of transforming the unequal social contract of civil society into "a form of association that defends and protects the person and property of each associate with all its common strength, and by which each, uniting with all, nevertheless obeys only himself and remains as free as before".

### The man/citizen distinction

Natural law is good for man, political law for the citizen. Through political law, the citizen commits to a project aimed at improving society. For Rousseau, taking part in a true social contract brings about a change of perspective that distinguishes man from citizen. Indeed, the citizen must learn to see himself as part of a whole, to listen to the voice of duty, to "consult his reason before listening to his inclinations". To unite citizens, so that they form a whole, Rousseau considers that having the same habits, beliefs and practices helps. Patriotism is also a means of binding citizens together and facilitating their acceptance of the general will. In this regard, Rousseau writes: "Love of country is the most effective; for as I have already said, every man is virtuous when his particular will conforms in everything to the general will, and we willingly want what the people we love want". We know that, for Rousseau, men are driven by two principles: self-love and pity. For the citizen, pity must give way to reciprocity. "The commitments that bind us to the social body are only binding because they are mutual".

**Equality, justice, utility and the body politic**

For Rousseau, the notion of justice is linked to reciprocity. The problem is that for there to be reciprocity, there must be equality. But since the end of the state of nature, natural freedom and equality have vanished. They must therefore be reconstituted by convention. In his project to reconstitute equality and freedom, Rousseau does not see equality as an end in itself, but as the means to secure the political freedom that can only exist between equals. While Rousseau is not opposed to inequalities resulting from human efforts, but rather to inequalities not justified by nature, he nevertheless considers equality to be always under threat, and sees its long-term establishment as a challenge that men must constantly take up. For him, political rights are based on people as they are, with their self-esteem, their interests, their views of the common good, which leads him to a relatively pragmatic approach. In *Du contrat social,* he writes:

"I will always try to combine, in this research, what the law allows with what the interest prescribes, so that justice and utility are not divided.

**The sovereignty of the people**

For Rousseau, the people, understood in the political sense of all citizens, are sovereign, meaning that they enact or ratify laws, and are the source of the general will. If they are sovereign, however, they do not govern and have no vocation to govern.

The question is how the sovereignty of the people can be exercised. There are two possible solutions: direct democracy or representative democracy. Rousseau was not very enthusiastic about representative democracy, preferring a form of direct democracy based on the ancient model. To confine oneself to voting is, in his view, to have a sovereignty that is only intermittent. He mocked the electoral system in use in England at the time, claiming that the people were free only on election day, and slaves as soon as their representatives were elected. His criticism of the idea of representation of the will is therefore severe:

Rousseau continues: "any law that the people themselves have not ratified is null and void; it is not a law". Christopher Bertram believes, however, that while the interpretation outlined above is the most widespread, it is not clear that it is correct, and that Rousseau really does reject all forms of representation as he implies.

Although Rousseau's vision of sovereignty differs from Hobbes's, as with the latter, by associating, citizens lose all their natural rights, in particular that of controlling sovereign power.

LA BOTANIQUE

DE

J. J. ROUSSEAU,

ORNÉE DE SOIXANTE-CINQ PLANCHES,

IMPRIMÉES EN COULEURS

D'APRÈS LES PEINTURES DE P. J. REDOUTÉ.

PARIS,

DELACHAUSSÉE, RUE DU TEMPLE, N.° 40;

GARNERY, RUE DE SEINE, N.° 6.

AN XIV. = 1805.

# Government

The sovereign, the people in Rousseau's view, promulgates the laws that are the expression of the general will. The government, by contrast, is a more limited body of people who administer the state within the framework of the laws. It is authorized to promulgate decrees implementing the laws in cases where this is necessary.

Rousseau insists on the necessary separation of government (the executive) and the legislature: the latter issues general laws, while the former executes them and adapts them to particular cases. Rousseau feared that mixing the executive and legislative branches would undermine the generality of the law. Moreover, the citizen of Geneva insists on the temptation of government to usurp sovereign (legislative) power. For Gourevitch, this fear raises the question of "to what extent are 'men as they are' and 'laws as they can be' reconcilable, even in the best of ordered societies?" and gives Rousseau's thought something of the insoluble, even the tragic.

**Three forms of government**

Rousseau distinguishes three types of government: pure or direct democracy, monarchy and aristocracy. Aristocracy can take three forms: natural, elective and hereditary. Direct democracy is best suited to small, virtuous states where equality of rank reigns. Rousseau was not really a fan of monarchy, which he felt favored the emergence of courtiers to the detriment of competent people. In financial terms, while direct democracy was concerned not to impose too many taxes on the people, this was not the case with monarchy, which he felt was only suitable for opulent nations. As for aristocracy, the hereditary model seems to him to be to be proscribed; as for natural aristocracy, he considers it possible only in small states. In his view, the best form of government is elective aristocracy, which he also calls temperate government. Speaking of elective aristocracy, Rousseau writes:

"But if aristocracy requires some virtues less than popular government, it also requires others that are peculiar to it: such as moderation in the rich and contentment in the poor; for it seems that rigorous equality would be out of place there; it was not even observed in Sparta."

**Civil religion**

Rousseau addresses this question in Book IV, Chapter 8 of the *Social Contract*. For him, the first political bodies were formed both by great figures who gave them their laws and by gods who, in a way, validated them by anointing them. As a result, the social contract acquired a transcendent dimension, prompting people to follow it out of fear of divine sanction. In his view, Christianity broke the link between religion and the body politic because it was concerned with people, not citizens. If Christianity spread the idea of natural law, by becoming a force, it divided the sovereignty of states. The citizen of Geneva therefore considers that Christian states do not practice what he calls sound politics. To re-establish the unity lost through Christianity, i.e. the opposition between religion and the local body politic, to "reunite the two heads of the eagle, and... bring everything back to political unity, without which neither state nor government will ever be well constituted", Rousseau proposes the creation of a civil religion based on a small number of positive dogmas, such as "the existence of a powerful, intelligent, beneficent, provident divinity, the life to come, the happiness of the just, the punishment of the wicked, the sanctity of the social contract and of laws".

**International law**

According to Rousseau, what he called the law of nations, and what we today would call international law, was a chimera. Indeed, he considered it difficult to "punish" a sovereign state. His own plans for a federation of European states and for a valid law of war remain fragmentary. Note that Rousseau sees war not as an opposition of individuals against one another, but as a struggle between moral entities, where state X fights state Y. The aim of war is not the death of a population, but to break the general will of the enemy state.

**Rousseau and botany**

Jean-Jacques Rousseau's work on botany includes numerous texts: *Lettres (élémentaires) sur la botanique à Madame Delessert* (1771 to 1774), an unfinished dictionary *Fragments pour un dictionnaire des termes d'usage en botanique* (1770), several manuscripts on botany, numerous herbariums and a rich correspondence with scholars from several European countries.

Faithful to the famous Swedish naturalist Carl von Linné, Rousseau nonetheless developed a naturalist philosophy of his own. "*I know of no study in the world better suited to my natural tastes than that of plants, and the life I have led for the last ten years in the country is little more than a continual herborization*" (The Confessions - Book V).

It was during his exile in Switzerland in 1762, at Môtiers in the canton of Neuchâtel, that Jean-Jacques Rousseau developed a passion for botany. He did so in the company of the Neuchâtel physician Jean-Antoine d'Ivernois, the notable Pierre-Alexandre DuPeyrou, the doctor Frédéric-Samuel Neuhaus and, above all, the naturalist Abraham Gagnebin, an excellent botanist. He built up his first herbarium and acquired botanical works to perfect his knowledge, based on Charles von Linné's Systema naturae, the reference work of the 18th$^{e}$ century. In a letter to François-Henri d'Ivernois in 1765, he confided, "*I'm crazy about botany: it's getting worse every day. I have nothing but hay in my head, I'm going to become a plant myself one of these mornings*" .

Driven out of Switzerland, Rousseau settled in England in 1766, in the small village of Wootton Hall. He met the Duchess of Portland, a botanical enthusiast, and continued to collect plants. He later sent her portable herbariums and kept up a long correspondence with her.

In particular, he corresponded with botanist Marc Antoine Louis Claret de la Tourrette, magistrate and botanist Chrétien-Guillaume de Lamoignon de Malesherbes and Abbé François Rozier. These exchanges enabled him to consolidate his mastery of plant identification.

Wherever he settled, he continued to collect, identify and sort, creating herbariums, notably at Grande-Chartreuse (1768), Maubec (1769), Mont-Pilat (1769) and Paris (1770 to 1778). A few weeks before his death in 1778, he produced his last herbarium plates at Ermenonville in the company of the son of the Marquis René-Louis de Girardin .

Rousseau's descriptions are both scientific: he takes maniacal care to describe flowers, petals and pistils, but they also reflect his love of nature. He was astonishingly inventive when he wrote lexicons of botanical terms in use at the time, or when he devised an ingenious system of "stenography" to transcribe them for more convenient herborizing.

Between 1771 and 1774, he wrote *Les Lettres (élémentaires) sur la botanique à Madame* Delessert to Madeleine-Catherine Delessert. A series of eight simple, methodical letters on botany, so that she could introduce her five-year-old daughter Madelon to the knowledge and love of flowers' . For Rousseau, it was as much a matter of learning "*to see well what the child is looking at", as of teaching her the nomenclature of flowers*". At the beginning of the XIX$^{e}$ century, these letters enjoyed European success, since until Rousseau, botanical books had been written by scientists for scientists.

**Jean-Jacques Rousseau and art**

Although Rousseau wrote a comedy, *Narcisse ou l'Amant de lui-même,* which was well received when it was presented at the Comédie-Française in 1752, he himself did not believe it to be a masterpiece. Because he had a triumph with *Le Devin du village*, a little opera of which Raymond Trousson says that while it is "not a great thing", it is delightful "and in line with his *Discours* [sur les sciences et les arts]". However, in what is his most famous writing on theater, the *Lettre à d'Alembert,* he is highly critical of the art form. This letter is primarily a response to the *Encyclopédie* article entitled *Genève*, in which D'Alembert argues for the creation of a theater. Rousseau felt provoked, believing that D'Alembert had been influenced by Voltaire, who owned property near Geneva. If we look beyond these sensitivities and stick to the facts, the project to establish a theater in Geneva pitted the city's Protestant high society in favor of the theater against ordinary citizens, whom Rousseau supported. This opposition has a political significance: Rousseau sees the theater as a social phenomenon that contributes to the alienation of the people and the destruction of public morals and freedom.

In his *Lettre à d'Alembert sur les spectacles*, Rousseau argues against the thesis of Cicero, Corneille, Racine, Voltaire and Diderot that an aesthetic object both gives pleasure and contributes to civilization by promoting virtue and provoking hatred of vice. For him, on the other hand, as Plato explains in chapter X of *The Republic*, art flatters the irrational part of the soul and does not educate. Indeed, he believes that a play must first and foremost please and flatter, preoccupations that annihilate any educational work. Moreover, Rousseau criticized the theater of his time for focusing on art for art's sake, and thus rejecting any social purpose.

Rousseau's criticism of the theater also ties in with that of what we would call today "the society of the spectacle", as court society can be analyzed as the first society of the spectacle. In Rousseau's view, theater in France developed within the framework of the monarchy, symbolizing both the pre-eminence of large cities over small towns, and that of the aristocracy who indulged in leisure over the working people. For the citizen of Geneva, the theater was part of the political institutions that perverted the people and made them evil. Generally speaking, Rousseau found the French art of his time too learned, too standardizing, or, to use a current expression, too "pensée unique". For him, culture varies from one people to another, and is particular, not uniform. So he felt that what might be appropriate in Paris could be harmful in Geneva.

Rousseau also disagrees with Diderot about the importance of acting. In his *Paradoxe sur le comédien,* Diderot appreciates actors' ability to play a role while remaining themselves. However, precisely what Diderot considers the pinnacle of the actor's art, of his virtuosity, Rousseau perceives, on the contrary, as the pinnacle of deception and duplicity.

In fact, for Rousseau, in a Republic, it's not theater that should be valued, but celebration:

"What! Doesn't a republic need shows? On the contrary, we need a lot of them! It's in republics that they are born... But what are the objects of these shows? What will they show? Nothing, if you like... Plant a picket crowned with flowers in the middle of a square, gather the people around it, and you'll have a festival."

## Rousseau and the novel: *The New Heloise*

In *The Confessions,* Rousseau argues that he wrote this novel to satisfy in fiction an irrepressible desire to love that he was unable to satisfy in reality' . In a way, this novel has a consoling value. He is also writing this novel because he believes that a work of fiction will enable his ideas to reach a wider, broader audience. What's more, he felt that, unlike theater, to which he had objected in *Lettre à D'Alembert,* a work of fiction was likely to make virtue lovable to everyone, because it featured ordinary people.

The plot of the novel is as follows. Saint-Preux, a tutor, falls in love with his pupil Julie d'Étange. Love is mutual, but financial and social constraints stand in the way of marriage. Saint-Preux is poor. So Julie marries Monsieur de Wolmar, a wealthy atheist thirty years her senior. In this novel, Rousseau introduces a separation between marriage and love. He believes that although M. and M$^{me}$ de Wolmar are not in love, they should remain united. He writes: "Whenever two spouses unite in a solemn knot, there is a tacit pledge by the whole human race to respect this sacred bond, to honor in them the conjugal union". While Leo Tolstoy, a great admirer of Rousseau, has Anna Karenina die while abandoning herself to her passion and leaving her husband, the Wolmar couple remain together. They found the community of Clarens, where gentleness and moderation reign. At the end of the story, however, Julie admits to having been a little bored during her marriage, and to not having forgotten Saint-Preux. The novel enjoyed considerable success in both the XVIII[e] and XIX centuries.[e]

**Language and literature**

The elegance of Rousseau's writing led to a significant transformation of French poetry and prose. In particular, it helped free them from the rigid standards of the Grand Siècle: "[Rousseau] was able to bring picturesque nature to life in his writings and awaken in the French a taste for natural beauty, inspiring in the literary generation that followed him a host of great painters of nature, the Bernardin de Saint-Pierre, the Chateaubriand, the Senancour, and above all his passionate pupil, George Sand".

Many writers outside France were also influenced by Rousseau. In Russia, for example, Pushkin and Tolstoy wrote: "At fifteen I wore around my neck a medallion with a portrait of Rousseau instead of the usual cross". In

England, he influenced Wordsworth, Coleridge, Lord Byron, Shelley and John Keats - in the United States, Hawthorne and Thoreau - in Germany, Goethe, Schiller and Herder. Schiller considered Rousseau his "guide", while Goethe remarked in 1787 that "*Emile ou De l'éducation* has had a notable influence on the cultivated minds of the world".

**Rousseau, composer and music critic**

Music was a thwarted vocation for Rousseau. Introduced to the practice of music by Madame de Warens, he made a mediocre living from it during his stay in Paris, essentially as a copyist - an activity to which he testifies in these terms: "As a man of letters, I have said all the bad things I think about my state; I have only made French music, and only like Italian; I have shown all the miseries of society when I was happy in it: as a bad copyist, I expose here what the good ones do. O truth! my interest was never anything before you; may it in no way sully the worship I have vowed to you".

Rousseau wrote an opera-ballet, *Les Muses galantes* - presented by the farmer-general La Pouplinière in 1743, then unsuccessfully at the Opéra in 1747 - and a melodrama entitled *Pygmalion*. According to François-Joseph Fétis, "Rousseau is the inventor of this kind of work, in which the orchestra dialogues with the words of the character on stage, and expresses the feelings he is moved by". The catalog of the philosopher-composer's works still includes fragments of a ballet on the theme of *Daphnis et Chloé*.

Music historians refer to *Le Devin du village* (1752), "a pastoral interlude whose tunes owe their naiveté only to their author's elementary musical knowledge". According to Paul Pittion, "the *Overture* is nothing more than a succession of dance tunes, but certain pages, such as Colin's aria *Je vais revoir ma charmante maîtresse*, and the couplets *L'art à l'amour est favorable,* are not without charm". This little opera was a real success: "it was sung by the whole of France, from Jéliotte and M^lle^ Fel to King Louis XV, who couldn't get enough of repeating *J'ai perdu mon serviteur*, with the falsest voice in his kingdom". The king offered Rousseau a pension, but he refused. It was at this point that Rousseau first quarreled with Diderot, who urged him to accept the royal offer.

Posterity has not been kind to Rousseau the composer. In his *Mémoires*, Hector Berlioz pitied "poor Rousseau, who attached as much importance to his score of Le *Devin du village* as to the masterpieces of eloquence that immortalized his name, and who firmly believed he had crushed the whole of Rameau, even the Trio des Parques, with the little songs, the little flon-flons, the little rondeaux, the little solos, the little bergeries, the little drolleries of all kinds of which his little interlude was composed".

In the history of French music, Rousseau is mainly remembered as a critic and opponent of Rameau, who considers him "a poor fool, who is not as evil as he is thought to be". Opera, which presented itself as "the glorious expression of the 'spectacle divertissement' as conceived by the aristocratic regime of Versailles", according to Jean Malignon, became the target of various quarrels, including the "Querelle des Bouffons", in which the Encyclopédistes pursued different goals: "through the pretextual curtain of the Opéra, Diderot aims at the very spirit of Versailles, Grimm aims at the entire French spirit, and Rousseau aims at a man".

In his *Lettre sur la musique française*, published in 1753, he attacks the author of *Hippolyte et Aricie* for his theories on harmony: "It is therefore a certain principle, founded in nature, that all music where harmony is scrupulously fulfilled, all accompaniment where all chords are complete, must make a lot of noise, but have very little expression: which is precisely the character of French music.

Rousseau concludes this *Letter* in a particularly trenchant manner, which provoked such a scandal that the actors and musicians of the Opéra burned the author in effigy in the courtyard of the Royal Academy of Music:

"I believe I have shown that there is neither measure nor melody in French music, because the language is not susceptible to them; that French song is nothing but a continual barking, unbearable to any untrained ear; that the harmony is crude, expressionless, and feeling only its schoolboy filling; that French airs are not airs; that French recitative is not recitative. From which I conclude that the French have no music and can have none, or that, if they ever do, it will be too bad for them.

For modern musicologists, Grimm's and Rousseau's attacks on Rameau's art "border on silliness". Berlioz came to regard Gluck's praise of Rousseau's music in the presence of Marie-Antoinette as "facetious perfidy". At the beginning of the XX$^{e}$ century, Claude Debussy still mocked "Jean-Jacques Rousseau's naïve aesthetic" and his "reasons - not very valid - for having a grudge against Rameau". One of his friends, the critic Louis Laloy, wrote: "For the citizen of Geneva, any music he cannot write himself is 'gothic'". In 1977, Antoine Goléa considered that the works of certain French composers, "the Philidors, the Monsignys, the Grétrys, would, in a pinch, justify Rousseau's placet, sublime in its ridiculousness", while criticizing the philosopher's retrograde attitude: "Rousseau thought of Rameau, thought of harmonic language and counterpoint, which he called 'a remnant of barbarism'. In Berlioz's time, he would have been for

Adam - in Debussy's time, for Saint-Saëns and Ambroise Thomas.

Considering the aesthetic evolution from lyric tragedy to opera, Jean Malignon nonetheless highlights the role of Rousseau the critic: "Let's leave aside for once his *Lettre sur la musique française*, quoted extensively - and, alas, exclusively - by Rameau historians, and open instead his *Lettre à d'Alembert sur les spectacles*. How biting! A masterpiece! With a single flick of his quill, he sweeps away all "these dressing-room weepers, so proud of their tears". A nice find, by the way! Unluckily, it's a work of bad humor", but one that provides "the key to a painful, inexplicable misunderstanding that for the whole of the XIX$^{e}$ century separated Rameau from the French public".

Indeed, "the soul that the Genevan Rousseau speaks of here represents something that was still quite rare at the time. Not even the way of pronouncing the word makes it sound new". François-Joseph Fétis also offers a nuanced portrait: "Without being a scholar in the theory and history of music, without having possessed a practical knowledge of harmony and counterpoint, without even having been a skilful enough reader to decipher a simple lesson in solfeggio, Jean-Jacques Rousseau exerted a great influence on the music of his time in France [...] In the aesthetics of music, moreover, he had correct, elevated views, and what he wrote about them was not without fruit for the reform of French taste in this art".

Rousseau is also considered one of the founders of ethnomusicology when, in his *Dictionnaire de musique*, he transcribes "two songs of the savages of America" to put the reader "within reach of judging the various musical accents of the Peoples".

**Contemporary questions on Rousseau's work**

Although Rousseau maintains that the fundamental unity of his work is based on the idea that man is naturally good, and that it is society that perverts him, the fact remains that until the beginning of the XX$^{e}$ century, Rousseau was read in a very dichotomous way: on the one hand, he was seen as a "magician of language", and on the other, as a man of contradictions whose case was almost pathological. It has to be said, however, that these were the more benevolent interpretations. According to Jean Starobinski, his accusers "held him guilty of all the political and moral disasters they saw coming in the modern world". It wasn't until the beginning of the XX$^{e}$ century that his political works were finally published in full, making it possible to read him systematically. Although Gustave Lanson was one of the first to insist on the unity of Rousseau's thought, it was Ernst Cassirer's analysis, set out in his 1932 book *Le problème Jean-Jacques Rousseau*, that made the unity thesis dominant, though not without encountering resistance. Against Cassirer, for example, Victor Basch argued in 1932 that Rousseau was first and foremost a poet, and that he "was only as much a thinker and philosopher as he was a poet and novelist". In his book *Anthropologie et politique. Les principes du système de Rousseau*, Victor Goldschmidt insists on the coherence of Rousseau's philosophical thought, which he believes results from the fact that the citizen of Geneva asserts that the same method must be used to analyze various disciplines, a method that is essentially based on "observation and reasoning".

At the beginning of the 21st$^{e}$ century, an author such as John Scott believes that while there are paradoxes in Rousseau's work, this does not mean that there is no unity. Indeed, the contradiction may only be the appearance of contradiction, waiting to be resolved. This author sees the work of the citizen of Geneva as an exposé of the system of man's natural goodness. However, in this maxim or conjecture, the adjective "good" does not mean that men are originally naturally virtuous and beneficent, but, according to John Scott, that in man "there would originally exist a balance between needs and passions and the capacity to satisfy them", and it would be this balance that would make man "good for himself and not dependent on others", for it is precisely "dependence on others that makes men bad".

*PRINCIPES*

DU

# DROIT POLITIQUE.

PAR J. J. ROUSSEAU,

*CITOYEN DE GENEVE.*

— *fœderis æquas*
*Dicamus leges.*
Æneid. xi.

*A AMSTERDAM,*

Chez MARC MICHEL REY.

MDCCLXII.

# Rousseau and feminism

Rousseau, in *Émile ou De l'éducation*, Book V, states: "To please men, to be useful to them, to be loved and honored by them, to bring them up young, to care for them as adults, to advise them, to console them, to make their lives pleasant and sweet, these are the duties of women in all times, and what they must be taught from childhood".

At the end of the XVIII^e century, Mary Wollstonecraft, one of the pioneers of feminism in England, denounced Rousseau's conception of woman as an intellectual sham, considering as nature that which is culture, an idea later developed by Simone de Beauvoir in her famous expression: "One is not born a woman, one becomes one". In her 1792 book, *A Vindication of the Rights of Woman,* translated as *Défense des droits de la femme,* she criticizes the philosopher of education's vision of woman, which denies women the very right to education. She suggests that, without this pernicious ideology that encourages young women to privilege their beauty and appearance, they could achieve far more fruitfully. Wives would be true companions, practicing a trade if they wished: "women could certainly study the art of healing and be doctors as well as nurses. They could also study politics [...] and hold all kinds of positions".

In *Lettre à d'Alembert sur les spectacles*, Rousseau writes "toute femme qui se montre se déshonore". Obliged to acknowledge that some women have talent, he specifies that this is "against his sentiment" and thus that "it is not to a woman but to women that he denies the talent of men". This assertion is part of a masculinist, even misogynist theory, but needs to be placed in the context of the times.

**Rousseau and the totalitarianism of the 20th$^{e}$ century**

As early as the XIX$^{e}$ century, Rousseau was the subject of criticism, such as that of Proudhon, for whom "the Revolution, the Republic and the people never had a greater enemy than Jean-Jacques",.

Bertrand Russell describes Rousseau, in his *History of Western Philosophy* (1952), as "the inventor of the political philosophy of pseudo-democratic dictatorships", and concludes that "Hitler is the result".

Although Rousseau repeatedly criticized the tyrannies and authoritarian regimes of his time, defending freedom of conscience and expression as the foundations of democracy, at least three authors (Marejko, Crocker and Talmon) have accused him of having influenced the emergence of totalitarianism. For Jan Marejko, this does not mean that Rousseau's writings are deliberately designed to create a totalitarian system. For the American academic Lester G. Crocker, two elements of Rousseau's thought are said to have favored contemporary totalitarianism: the autarkic tendency of Rousseau's thought, and his insistence on the idea of national unity (criticized in his day by Abbé Bergier, who spoke of "fanatical patriotism"). Israeli historian Jacob L. Talmon also sees in Rousseau's theory of the general will the origin of what he calls "totalitarian democracy".

Leo Strauss opposes this interpretation, believing, as Céline Spector puts it, "that the Rousseauist contract cannot require the sacrifice of the individual, since nature dictates nothing other than self-interest". According to Strauss, "Rousseau believed that revolutions could restore the moderation of antiquity on new, conscious principles. His thought is a bizarre union of the radical, revolutionary progressivism of modernity and the discretion and reserve of antiquity".

In France, the Vichy regime was divided in its appreciation of Rousseau. Marcel Déat hailed a "totalitarian Jean-Jacques Rousseau", socialist and national. Among the more Maurrasian members, the citizen of Geneva was sometimes portrayed as the very figure of the "wandering Jew" or, even by Maurras himself, as an "individualist anarchist" and "false prophet". In a book on Montesquieu published in 1943, M. Duconseil, a supporter of Pétain's "National Revolution" and collaborator with *L'Action française*, wrote: "Jean-Jacques Rousseau is the great Semitic figure who dominates our time. [He is the father of modern democratic dogmas". Dominique Sordet likens Rousseau to Léon Blum, and describes the philosopher's ideas as "destructive [...] of any hierarchical, and therefore Aryan, social order".

Bruno Bernardi points out that in the *Social Contract,* "the sovereignty of citizens is the sole foundation of the obedience of subjects. The consistency of sovereignty depends on the obedience of subjects. It is only at the cost of disarticulating this double constraint, which in Rousseau's eyes was inseparable, and of confusing the subject and the citizen, that we can see the seeds of a totalitarian conception of the State [...]". He notes that

"Rousseau] has been seen as both an apostle of the irreducible freedom of the individual and a purveyor of totalitarianism. In its very excessiveness, this opposition refers back to the characterization of his epistemological approach: it has been possible to attribute to him both an individualistic and a holistic orientation. Should his conception of society be seen as the implementation of an artificialist, mechanistic or organicist model? Without overlapping, these three interpretative debates obviously relate to each other. If the most attentive exegetes of Rousseau's thought have refused to accept any one-sided reading, if L.-J. Talmon's totalitarian Rousseau [...] has hardly seemed credible to them, they generally seem to accept the terms of the debate. [...] Doesn't a careful reading of this chapter [*Du contrat social/Edition 1762/Book I/Chapter 5* (Wikisource)] show that Rousseau is precisely seeking to free himself from the opposition between organicism and mechanistic artificialism?"

**Leo Strauss's interpretation of Rousseau's thought**

Alongside Machiavelli, Hobbes and Tocqueville, Rousseau is one of Leo Strauss's favorite authors. For this philosopher, the Citizen of Geneva marks the beginning of the second wave of modernity. The first wave began with Machiavelli and Hobbes, while the third began with Friedrich Nietzsche. While the first wave turned morality and politics into a technical problem, Rousseau, on the other hand, sought to give them a non-technical place, without returning to the classics. Strauss interprets the notion of the general will as an extension of the particular will, as a prefiguration of Kant's categorical imperative. The general will, he argues, is "a necessary constraint" to the good life in society. Strauss focuses on Rousseau's *Discours sur les sciences et les arts,* which he analyzes as a move away from an Enlightenment conception of science as a substitute for religion, as a means of leading people to happiness. According to Strauss, for Rousseau,

"Science is bad, not in the absolute, but only for the people or for society; it is good, and even necessary, for the few among whom Rousseau counts himself."

According to Leo Strauss, while the laws of the general will are dependent on the legislator, and always contain an element of mystery, philosophy seeks to bring this mystery to light, and thus make it lose its own effectiveness: "In other words," he notes, "society must do everything possible to make citizens forget the very facts that political philosophy focuses on, as constituting the foundations of society. Society stakes its existence on a specific blindness against which philosophy necessarily revolts".

**Rousseau as seen by Habermas (school of Critical Theory)**

Habermas, in *L'Espace public: archéologie de la publicité comme dimension constitutive de la société bourgeoise*, considers Rousseau to be one of the first to have thought about the role of public opinion. According to the German philosopher, the citizen of Geneva "links the general will to a public opinion that coincides with thoughtless and spontaneous opinion, with opinion as it is published"' . In this respect, he notes that Rousseau speaks out against lengthy debates, which he sees as weakening the social bond. In Rousseau, public opinion exercises a certain power of direction (Habermas recalls that Rousseau writes in *Du contrat social* (book IV, ch.7) "public opinion is the species of law of which the censor is the minister", but that in Rousseau, this public opinion is "channeled" by the legislator who translates the general will into law). On these points, Habermas differs from Rousseau in insisting on the deliberative aspect, so that, for him, "the general will is ... discursively formed, in the space of public discussion". There is another point of disagreement between Habermas and Rousseau. Whereas the citizen of Geneva insists on the notion of patrie, and assumes a relatively homogeneous community that shares respect for the same virtues, the same conception of the good of the community, Habermas, who believes that these conditions cannot be fulfilled in a non-homogeneous society, proposes for the world of the XXI$^{e}$ century "a model of political integration, insisting on the procedural conditions of opinion and will formation".

J. JAQUES ROUSSEAU.

# Influence

Rousseau's thought influenced both the French Revolution and the republicanism of the Third Republic in France. Philosophically, Rousseau had a strong influence on German philosophy, but he was contested by liberals and certain Marxists, while he was appreciated by the urbaphobic current.

**Influence on the French Revolution**

Royalist Charles Maurras sees Rousseau as the inspiration behind the Revolution, and the intellectual source of all France's ills:

Here, Maurras takes up a counter-revolutionary tradition initiated by Edmund Burke, Joseph de Maistre, author of *Examen d'un écrit de J.-J. Rousseau sur l'inégalité des conditions parmi les hommes*, published posthumously as *Contre Rousseau*, and Louis de Bonald.

Scholars who have studied the question take a more nuanced and documented approach. For George Armstrong Kelly, before the Revolution, Rousseau was best known as the author of the *Emile* and the *Discourses*. It was only after the start of the Revolution that his political writings were really discovered by Sieyès, Marat and others. What struck revolutionaries early on was

Rousseau's idea that man had distanced himself from nature, leading to slavery and its aftermath. It's also the idea that, like Sparta and Rome, people sometimes have the right to a second birth. It was this Rousseauist scenario that profoundly influenced the Montagnards, notably Robespierre and Saint-Just. Where Rousseau saw masters and slaves, the proponents of the French Revolution insisted on the hidden nature of the French people, preserved from the depravity of the Ancien Régime. For George Armstrong Kelly, Rousseau's Montagnard followers transformed Rousseau's pervasive notion of memory into a desire for a new beginning, with new heroes and a new city. A desire to return to the time when man was good.

Jean Starobinski illustrates Rousseau's "political conservatism" by quoting his *Judgement on Polysynody. O.C.* (1756), III, 638 :

"Let us judge the danger of once moving the enormous masses that make up the French monarchy! Whether the present government is still the same as in the past, or whether over so many centuries it has insensitively changed its nature, it is equally imprudent to touch it. If it is the same, it must be respected; if it has degenerated, it is by the force of time and of things, and human wisdom can do nothing about it".

Jean Starobinski believes that "in this respect, Rousseau's thinking is very similar to that of Montesquieu. The same caution, the same choice between preserving the primitive institution and degenerating it, the same reluctance to take action in the name of progress...". Further on, this time commenting on the *Social Contract* (1762), he adds:

"Rousseau is certainly sincere when he denies having wanted to disturb the established order and overthrow the institutions of monarchical France. In *Lettres de la Montagne* (I^re^ partie, lettre VI), he asserts that the *Contrat social,* far from proposing the image of a city that would supplant existing society, merely describes what the republic of Geneva was like before the troubles that corrupted it. In the *Confessions,* the *Contract is* presented as a work of abstract reflection, for which Rousseau did not "seek application". He merely made full use of the "right to think" that men universally possess."

For Jean Starobinski: "If it is true that Rousseau's thought is revolutionary, we must immediately add that it is so in the name of eternal human nature, and not in the name of historical progress (Rousseau's work must be 'interpreted' to be seen as a decisive factor in the political progress of the 18th^e^ century)".

**Arendt's critique of Rousseau's influence on the French Revolution**

Arendt's criticism of Rousseau focuses on two points. On the one hand, she argues, Rousseau identifies sovereignty with power, and on the other, gives pity a political role. She strongly emphasizes the second point. For her, it was the primacy given to the social question that prevented the Revolution from instituting freedom. This emphasis on pity comes from Rousseau, the first to give importance to this emotion. She writes: "He was more interested in his own emotion than in the suffering of others, he delighted in emotions and moods as they revealed themselves to him in the exquisite delights of intimacy that Rousseau was the first to discover". For Arendt, the problem lies in the fact that pity is not a constructive political sentiment, especially when, like the men of the Revolution, it is taken for a virtue and Montesquieu's precept that even virtue must have limits is disbelieved. For Arendt, in politics, it's not pity, but the solidarity that comes from reason that makes things better.

**Rousseau and the republican tradition in France**

Claude Nicolet, in *L'idée républicaine en France* (1982), a book that contributed to the resurgence of republicanism in the 1980s, argues that it was Rousseau who provided the theoretical foundation for the notion of republic as understood in France. According to this author, the republican idea in France was built around the concepts of sovereignty and the theory of law developed by the citizen of Geneva. Nicolet writes:

"Rousseau is, of course, the great concern of republicans. The man and the work were, in themselves, so intimately linked, so contradictory in appearance, and so coherent in reality, that it's hardly surprising that Rousseau was, for a century - and perhaps more - both the inevitable reference and the most striking sign of division among French republicans, as well as a few others' ."

More generally, Rousseau is considered, along with Kant and positivism, to be one of the three "sources" of republican doctrine in France. He gave republicans historical legitimacy in the face of monarchists and Catholics. However, this legacy poses the problem of how to interpret the *Social Contract*, which pits a Rousseau in favor of aristocratic government against the more republican Rousseau claimed by Robespierre. For Nicolet, Rousseau is not a democratic author in the contemporary sense, as Mme de Staël and Benjamin Constant have believed, because he retains the ancient meaning of republic as a legitimate state governed by laws, which owes much to Aristotelian *politeia.* According to this interpretation, "Rousseau's legacy would be threefold: beyond the prince of popular sovereignty and the definition of law as an expression of the general will, the philosopher's work would have inspired a theory of virtue as a goal of general interest, deemed consubstantial with republicanism".

Rousseau was absent from the revival of republican thought initiated by Quentin Skinner and John Pocock in the 1960s and 1970s. This revival, which rejects the dualism introduced by Isaiah Berlin between positive and negative freedom, is more in the wake of Cicero than Aristotle, and in the republican tradition of Machiavelli. For them, individual freedom resides first and foremost in participation in political institutions.

**Rousseau and the concept of sovereignty**

In a study of the concept of sovereignty, Jacques Maritain sees in "the myth of the *General Will*" expounded in *Du contrat social* "a means of transferring to the people the separate and transcendent power of the absolute king." Yet, according to the philosopher, this transfer is highly problematic:

"Thus Rousseau, who was not a democrat, introduced into the nascent modern democracies a notion of Sovereignty that was destructive of democracy, and tended towards the totalitarian state. [...] The Lawgiver, the superman described in the *Social Contract*, offers us a foretaste of our modern totalitarian dictators whose "great soul is the true miracle that must prove" their "mission", and who must "alter the constitution of man in order to strengthen it" (II, iv). Didn't Rousseau believe, moreover, that the State has the right of life and death over the citizen?"

And Maritain concludes: "Rousseau's State is but Hobbes's Leviathan crowned by the General Will, in place of the crown of those whom the Jacobin vocabulary called *kings and tyrants.*"

For his part, Alain de Benoist states:

"Whereas the philosophers of the Enlightenment sought to limit the prerogatives of power and challenged the very notion of *sovereignty,* Rousseau made sovereignty the cornerstone of his entire political system. Calling the body politic to which the social contract gives rise the sovereign, he deduced that the general will being one, the resulting sovereignty could not be fragmented without losing all meaning. By definition, sovereignty cannot be divided. Rousseau therefore rejects any separation of powers, any attempt to divide sovereignty. The contrast with liberal proposals is striking. Rousseau rejects the alternative between liberalism and despotism, or rather he believes that by establishing the citizen, we can ensure political and social unity without falling into despotism. It could be said that, in the final analysis, Rousseau simply wanted to change the monarch: he substituted the people for the king of divine right, but without ever abandoning the idea of absolute sovereignty. That said, he was fairly indifferent to the *form of* government. He is not hostile, for example, to aristocratic government, which he even expressly calls "the best form of government". But this must be understood within his system. For Rousseau, what's essential is that the people hold legislative power and never relinquish it. Once this has been achieved, *executive* power can just as easily take an aristocratic form. The ability to govern is not the same as sovereignty.

**Influence on liberalism**

In 1788, Madame de Staël published her *Lettres sur l'œuvre et le caractère de J.-J. Rousseau*, in which she criticized Rousseau. Benjamin Constant makes Rousseau one of those responsible for the Terror, for failing to set limits on popular sovereignty. Hegel, starting from a different premise - not having placed the general will at the service of the state, seen as possessing something divine, but at the service of civil society - also arrives, like Constant, at the conclusion that Rousseau is responsible for the Terror.

Constant also criticized Rousseau for having stuck to the politically-oriented freedom of the ancients, and for having failed to consider the freedom of the moderns, more oriented towards the individual and economic sphere. At the end of the XIX$^{e}$ century, beginning of the XX$^{e}$ century, liberals such as Émile Faguet and Léon Duguit criticized Rousseau for having sacrificed the individual to the State. Duguit was already making the accusation that Rousseau was the father of tyranny. In *Souveraineté et liberté (*1921), he wrote that Rousseau was "the initiator of all doctrines of dictatorship and tyranny, from the Jacobin doctrines of 1793 to the Bolshevik doctrines of 1920". This criticism was taken up again during the Cold War, when Rousseau was seen by a liberal like Jacob Leib Talmon as one of the fathers of totalitarianism. Friedrich Hayek associated Rousseau with constructivism. In Volume 2 of *Law, Legislation and Liberty (chapter 11, page 178)*, he writes:

"Nostalgia for a Rousseau-like society guided not by moral laws learned and justiciable only by intellectual grasp of the principles on which this order is founded, but by the unthinking "natural" emotions rooted in millennia of living in small hordes - this nostalgia leads directly to calling for a socialist society where authority enforces visible "social justice" in a way that suits these natural emotions."

According to Christopher Bertram, the liberal political philosophy of John Rawls, particularly that of his major work The *Theory of Justice*, bears certain similarities to the thought of Rousseau. In particular, the way Rawls introduces the notion of original position to place self-interest at the service of principles of justice is reminiscent of Rousseau's argument that citizens should be chosen by lot to select laws impartially.

**Influence on German philosophy**

Rousseau influenced Kant, who had a portrait of himself as the only ornament on his desk. It is also said that the only exception the latter made to his ritual daily walk was the day he was too absorbed in reading the *Emile he had* just received. For Bertram, Rousseau's notion of the general will permeates the notion of the categorical imperative, notably in the third formulation found in Foundations of the Metaphysics of Morals. However, Rousseau's thinking is opposed to the Kantian idea of universal legislation. Indeed, in his preparatory work for the Social Contract, the famous Genevese rejected the idea of a general will of mankind. For him, the general will appears only in the context of the state. Rousseau's influence on Kant can also be seen in his moral psychology, notably in his book *Religion within the Limits of Simple Reason*.

The relationship between Rousseau and Hegel is equally complex. While in Philosophy of Right, Hegel congratulates Rousseau on seeing the will as the basis of the state, he misconceives the notion of the general will, which he sees as covering the contingent wills of individuals. Finally, Hegel takes up Rousseau's notion of self-love, as well as the idea that expecting respect and exact recognition from others can lead to submission.

Schopenhauer, for his part, said: "My theory has the authority of the greatest of modern moralists.J. Rousseau, who knew the human heart so thoroughly, who drew his wisdom not from books but from life, who produced his doctrine not for the pulpit but for humanity, this enemy of prejudice, this infant of nature, who inherited from his mother the gift of moralizing without boring, because he possessed the truth and moved hearts.

As far as Karl Marx is concerned, while the ideas of alienation and exploitation can be seen as having certain links with Rousseau's thinking on these subjects, references to Rousseau in Marx's work are too rare, and of too little importance, to really draw any definite conclusions.

**Rousseau, socialism, Marxism**

Rousseau's political thought influenced the revolutionaries of 1830 and 1848, Blanqui and the Communards of 1871, as well as the anarchists of the late 19th century.[e]

Liberal economist Frédéric Bastiat saw Saint-Simon, Charles Fourier and their followers as the "sons of Rousseau". Similarly, for the socialist Jean Jaurès, Rousseau was the precursor of socialism. Célestin Bouglé, for his part, believes that Rousseau's theory of laws "opens the way directly to socialism".

Rousseau's emphasis on social antagonisms arising from the division of labor and private property also makes him a precursor of Marxism. Yet Marx quotes Rousseau very sparingly. When he does refer to part of chapter 7 of Book II of the *Social Contract, it's in a* negative way, noting that it's "an excellent picture of bourgeois abstraction". In fact, Karl Marx criticizes Rousseau for not taking social relations sufficiently into account. Generally speaking, Marxists, particularly in the 1960s, favored a reading of the *Social Contract* over the *Second Discourse*, and were highly critical of the notion of the general will. In their view, the general will is opposed to the Marxist reading in terms of class struggle and political conflict.

In Italy, Rousseau was studied by Galvano Della Volpe, a disciple of Gramsci. Initially, in 1945, this author argued that Rousseau was opposed to Marxism as a continuator of a tradition "that starts from Plato and, through Christianity, joins secular jusnaturalism". In 1954, on the other hand, he argued that Locke and Rousseau had given rise to two theories of democracy: "a Locke-Kant-Humboldt-Constant line, which produced the theory of liberal democracy; and a Rousseau-Marx-Engels-Lenin line, which found its historical incarnation in Soviet democracy (proletarian and non-representative)". Under these conditions, Rousseau could, in his view, have contributed to enriching Marxism.

Marxism at the beginning of the XXI$^{e}$ century, as developed around Toni Negri, is highly critical of Rousseau, whom it sees as one of the thinkers of sovereignty - a concept it deems reactionary - and as the promoter of a juridical vision that encourages an organizational, even bureaucratic orientation of power and society.

J. J. ROUSSEAU,
AUTHOR OF LETTERS ON BOTANY, &c.

### Rousseau and the "urbaphobic" movement

Rousseau is considered one of the founders of the "urbaphobic" movement against the big city. In l'*Émile*, Rousseau describes his ideal, the isolated farmhouse living self-sufficiently under a patriarchal regime: "The linen comes from his hemp, spun in winter by his wife, his daughters and his servant; no hands other than those of his family have made the preparations for his table; the nearest mill and the neighboring market are the limits of the universe for him".

### Rousseau as the founder of anthropology

Claude Lévi-Strauss declared that Rousseau "didn't just foresee ethnology: he founded it".

Lévi-Strauss first emphasizes Rousseau's anthropological project, which seeks to distinguish the contribution of nature and culture to the functioning of human societies. Lévi-Strauss also emphasizes Rousseau's injunction to travel in order to gain a better understanding of being, an injunction generally taken up by ethnology. Levi-Strauss quotes Rousseau:

"When you want to study men, you have to look close to yourself; but to study man, you have to learn to look far away; you first have to observe the differences to discover the properties. (Rousseau, Essai sur l'origine des langues, ch. VIII.)"

Lévi-Strauss also notes that Rousseau deplored his contemporaries' lack of interest in studying cultures and customs, preferring to travel to study stones and plants rather than people.

For Lévi-Strauss, the introspection that characterizes Rousseau's thought is also one of his influences on anthropological thought. According to Lévi-Strauss, since the observer is his or her own instrument of observation in ethnographic experience, he or she must be particularly introspective to avoid bias. Lévi-Strauss thus contrasts Rousseau's thinking with that of Descartes, where the latter "believes he passes directly from the interiority of a man to the exteriority of the world, without seeing that between these two extremes lie societies, civilizations, that is, worlds of men".

# Tributes to Rousseau and his presence in popular culture

**France's tribute: the transfer to the Panthéon**

The question of the nation's tribute to Rousseau arose shortly after the Assembly's decision on April 4, 1791 to transform the church of Sainte-Geneviève into a burial ground for great men, following Voltaire's entry into what had become the Pantheon on July 11, 1791. In August 1791, the journalist and writer Pierre-Louis Ginguené drew up a petition which he circulated among literary circles. Backed by 300 signatures, it was submitted by two deputations, one of Parisians, the other of Montmorency residents. The Parisians demanded not only a statue, but also a transfer to the Pantheon, while the Montmorency inhabitants were content with a cenotaph in the Republican memorial.

The project lay dormant for several years. On April 11, 1794, Thérèse, widow of Rousseau, appeared before the National Convention to firmly demand the promised transfer. The events of the Terror further delayed the implementation of the decision. Finally, the ceremony was set for October 11, 1794.

The entrance to the Panthéon is accompanied by the sound of the organ, in "religious contemplation". Cambacérès, President of the Convention, eulogized the great man:

"A profound moralist and apostle of liberty and equality, he was the precursor who called the nation onto the road to glory and happiness. [...] It is to Rousseau that we owe this salutary regeneration, which has brought about such happy changes in our manners, our customs, our laws, our spirits, our habits... This day, this apotheosis, this gathering of an entire people, this triumphal pomp, all announce that the Convention wishes to pay both to the philosopher of nature, and the debt of the French people, and the gratitude of humanity."

The ceremony ends with Marie-Joseph Chénier's *Hymne à Jean-Jacques Rousseau, set to* music by Gossec. In the evening, the people dance. An engraving by Geissler depicts the *Resurrection of Jean-Jacques Rousseau* where, wearing his Armenian cap, he emerges from the tomb like a new Christ. A one-act comic opera by Dalayrac, with libretto by Andrieux, entitled *L'Enfance de Jean-Jacques Rousseau*, premiered on May 23, 1794 and was performed until 1796.

### Jean-Jacques Rousseau Museum in Montmorency

The Musée Jean-Jacques Rousseau is located in Montmorency, in the Val-d'Oise region of France. In April 1756, Jean-Jacques Rousseau fled Paris, "a *city of noise, smoke and mud*", and settled in Montmorency, at a place called "L'Hermitage". In December 1757, he and Térèse Levasseur moved into what is now the Musée Jean-Jacques Rousseau at Petit Mont-Louis.

From 1757 to 1762, in the "Donjon" that was his study, he wrote his major works: Julie ou la Nouvelle Héloïse, Lettre à d'Alembert sur les spectacles de l'Encyclopédie, Émile, ou De l'éducation and Du contrat social. The condemnation of Emile in Paris caused the philosopher to flee Montmorency on June 9, 1762.

The Musée Jean-Jacques Rousseau comprises the Petit Mont-Louis, the philosopher's house, the Maison des Commères, the "Donjon" and a garden including the Cabinet de Verdure. The museum houses documents relating to Rousseau's life and work, and boasts a collection of some 12,000 items. Housed in a 17th$^{e}$ century building, the Rousseauist studies library contains some 30,000 documents.

### Maison des Charmettes in Chambéry

It was in the Charmettes valley on the outskirts of Chambéry, in an unspoilt natural setting, that Rousseau met his first love and benefactress, Madame de Warens, between 1736 and 1742. In the house that once belonged to Madame de Warens, an atmospheric museum has been created. The house has retained its Savoyard character, with a gable roof. On the first floor are the dining room, music room and library. Upstairs, the bedrooms of Madame de Warens and Jean-Jacques have been reconstructed. Adjacent to the house is a French-style terraced garden inspired by the 18th$^{e}$ century, featuring four planting squares.

Ever since Rousseau's death and the French Revolution, the house at Les Charmettes has been a place of pilgrimage. A period of formation and happiness, the Charmettes allowed Rousseau to become himself. It was the source of his "storehouse of ideas" (Les Confessions, Book VI), and has become a place of cultural tourism.

**Musée Jacquemart-André in Fontaine-Chaalis**

The Musée Jacquemart-André at Challis Abbey presents 6,000 works of art, furniture, paintings, sculptures and decorative objects. It is housed in the château built by Jean Aubert in the 18th century, next to the remains of an ancient Cistercian abbey dating from the 12th$^{e}$ century, in the heart of a magnificent park.

The Galerie Rousseau houses the important collection of the Marquis René-Louis de Girardin, who welcomed

Rousseau in 1778 for the last six weeks of his life. The ensemble comprises some 400 objets d'art, over 500 manuscripts (including the only known autograph score of Les Muses galantes), herbariums, personal objects that belonged to Jean-Jacques Rousseau (his inkwell, cane and armchair), 600 books from the Rousseau library and busts of Voltaire and Rousseau by Jean-Antoine Houdon .

**The Rousseau trail at his birthplace in Geneva**

The Parcours Rousseau is located in the house where the writer was born, at N° 40, Grand-Rue in Geneva's Old Town, at the heart of the "Maison Rousseau et Littérature". It features seven thematic niches (Happiness, Geneva, Sentiment, Liberty, Childhood, Nature and Multiple Faces), designed as a promenade confronting Rousseau's work and ideas with the concerns of our time.

**Môtiers Museum**

The Musée Rousseau de Môtiers is housed in the house occupied by Jean-Jacques Rousseau and Marie-Thérèse Levasseur during their years of exile from 1762 to 1765 in Môtiers, in the canton of Neuchâtel. All that remains of the XV^e^ century building is Rousseau's bedroom and kitchen. Transformed into a museum, it presents little-known aspects of the philosopher's life and work, in particular his Neuchâtel exile.

**Geneva public and university libraries**

The Bibliothèque de Genève is one of Switzerland's oldest and most important heritage and encyclopedic libraries, founded in 1559. The Salle Rousseau houses some of the philosopher's rarest manuscripts, including one of the first drafts of Du Contrat social, known as the Geneva manuscript. Also on display are the first draft of the Dictionnaire de musique and the autograph manuscript of the first part of the Confessions (written between 1764 and 1770) and the Rêveries du promeneur solitaire. The iconography center also boasts one of the world's largest collections of iconography.

**Neuchâtel public and university libraries**

The University Public Library was founded in Neuchâtel in 1778. It benefits from the archives of Pierre-Alexandre DuPeyrou, Rousseau's friend and protector. Along with Geneva, the Espace Rousseau boasts the finest collection of Rousseau's manuscripts. The exhibition focuses on the Neuchâtel years (1762-1765). Manuscripts on display include correspondence, texts on music and botany, autograph copies, drafts and manuscripts of Lettres écrites de la Montagne, Confessions and Rêveries du promeneur solitaire.

In 2011, the Neuchâtel Public and University Library's collection joined the Geneva Library's collection on UNESCO's Memory of the World international register.

LES
POESIES
DU
S.R ROUSSEAU
TOM. III.

OEUVRES
DIVERSES
DE
M^R. ROUSSEAU.
NOUVELLE EDITION,
Revue, corrigée & considerablement augmentée par lui-même
TOME TROISIEME

A AMSTERDAM,
Chez FRANÇOIS CHANGUION,
M. DCC. XXXIV.

# Tributes from Geneva

Geneva's Île Rousseau is named after the city's native philosopher of the Enlightenment. The island was known as Île aux Barques before taking on its new name in 1834. The following year, in 1835, a statue of Rousseau was erected on the island by sculptor James Pradier. Previously, more discreet tributes in the form of busts had adorned the Parc des Bastions, such as the one created by Jean Jaquet in 1793, then the marble one created by James Pradier, inaugurated on April 30, 1821, and now housed in Geneva's Musée d'art et d'histoire.

Rousseau's relationship with his hometown was tumultuous: in June 1762, his works *Du contrat social* and *Discours sur l'origine et les fondements de l'inégalité parmi les hommes were* burnt by the Geneva government. However, according to the city of Geneva's website, "The Bibliothèque de Genève today houses the philosopher's rarest manuscripts, including one of the first drafts of *Du contrat social*, known as the Geneva manuscript", as well as important documentation. Together with the Bibliothèque publique et universitaire de Neuchâtel, these are the two institutions in Switzerland with the rarest works by Rousseau. As a result, Switzerland will be included in UNESCO's "Memory of the World" register in 2011.

In 1969, a post-compulsory education building was opened in Geneva's Bouchet district, bearing the name Collège Rousseau, in homage to the author of the famous work on education entitled *L'Émile*.

Geneva celebrated the tercentenary of Rousseau's birth in 2012, with an event called "2012 Rousseau pour tous". It lasted a year and featured "exhibitions, shows, opera, concerts, republican banquets, films, walks, publications and symposia". 2012 also saw the creation of the *Maison de Rousseau et de la Littérature* in Geneva. It is essentially a place for meetings and debates.

# Other books by United Library

https://campsite.bio/unitedlibrary

Milton Keynes UK
Ingram Content Group UK Ltd.
UKHW020111211223
434710UK00018B/592